SCRATCH & PLAY®
Holiday
HANGMAN

Mike Ward

PUZZLE
WRIGHT
PRESS

New York

PUZZLE
WRIGHT
PRESS

New York

An Imprint of Sterling Publishing
387 Park Avenue South
New York, NY 10016

PUZZLEWRIGHT PRESS and the distinctive Puzzlewright Press logo
are registered trademarks of Sterling Publishing Co., Inc.

© 2012 by Mike Ward, Brainteaser Publications

ISBN 978-1-4027-9447-6

Distributed in Canada by Sterling Publishing
ᶜ/₀ Canadian Manda Group, 165 Dufferin Street
Toronto, Ontario, Canada M6K 3H6
Distributed in the United Kingdom by GMC Distribution Services
Castle Place, 166 High Street, Lewes, East Sussex, England BN7 1XU
Distributed in Australia by Capricorn Link (Australia) Pty. Ltd.
P.O. Box 704, Windsor, NSW 2756, Australia

For information about custom editions, special sales, premium and corporate purchases,
please contact Sterling Special Sales at 800-805-5489 or specialsales@sterlingpublishing.com.

Printed in China

2 4 6 8 10 9 7 5 3 1

www.puzzlewright.com

How to Play Hangman

It's simple, easy, and fun. Your goal is to fill in the missing letters at the bottom of each puzzle before the body in the gallows is completed. Scratch the silver oval below one of the letters of the alphabet. (Note: it's best not to leave the book in the sun, which may cause the ovals to become dry and harder to scratch off.) If the letter you guessed is correct, a number—or more than one number—will tell you where to enter this letter in the word or words below. If you are wrong, you'll see a bold ✖ to indicate that your guess is incorrect (you'll just have to imagine the game-show-style buzzer sound effect), in which case you must fill in one of the dotted lines on the body in the gallows.

There are six parts to the body—two arms, two legs, the torso, and the head. If you find all the letters in the complete word or phrase before you have to fill in six body parts, you win! If not ....

Good luck!

—Mike Ward

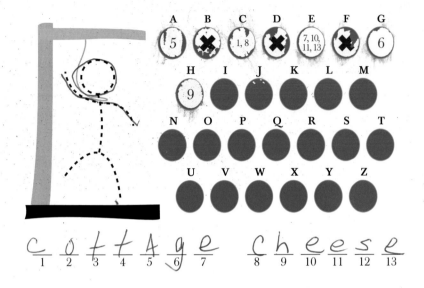

A	B	C	D	E	F	G
5	✖	1, 8	✖	7, 10, 11, 13	✖	6

H	I	J	K	L	M
9					

N	O	P	Q	R	S	T

U	V	W	X	Y	Z

c o t t a g e   c h e e s e
1 2 3 4 5 6 7   8 9 10 11 12 13

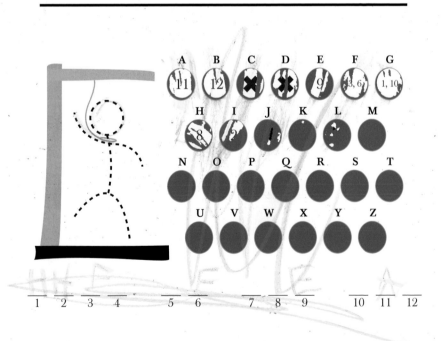

A	B	C	D	E	F	G
11	12	✖	✖	9	3, 6	1, 10

H	I	J	K	L	M
8	5	7			

N	O	P	Q	R	S	T

U	V	W	X	Y	Z

1 2 3 4   5 6   7 8 9   10 11 12

4

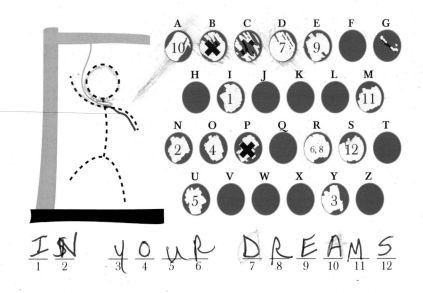

IN YOUR DREAMS

1 2 3 4 5 6 7 8 9 10 11 12

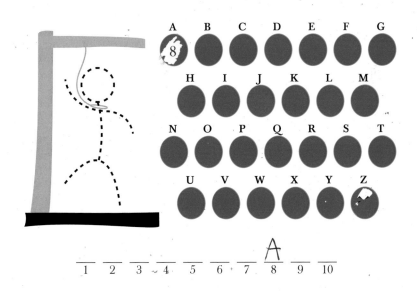

1 2 3 4 5 6 7 8 9 10

A
(at position 8)

5

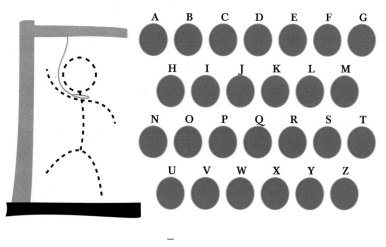

A	B	C	D	E	F	G
H	I	J	K	L	M	
N	O	P	Q	R	S	T
U	V	W	X	Y	Z	

‾1‾ ‾2‾ ‾3‾ ‾4‾ ‾5‾ ‾6‾ ‾7‾ ‾8‾ ‾9‾ ‾10‾ ‾11‾ ‾12‾ ‾13‾ ‾14‾

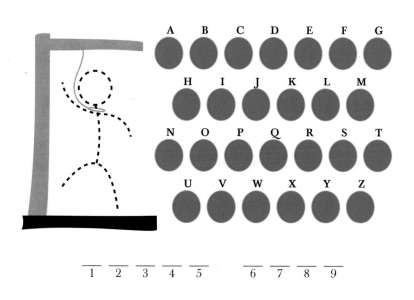

A	B	C	D	E	F	G
H	I	J	K	L	M	
N	O	P	Q	R	S	T
U	V	W	X	Y	Z	

‾1‾ ‾2‾ ‾3‾ ‾4‾ ‾5‾   ‾6‾ ‾7‾ ‾8‾ ‾9‾

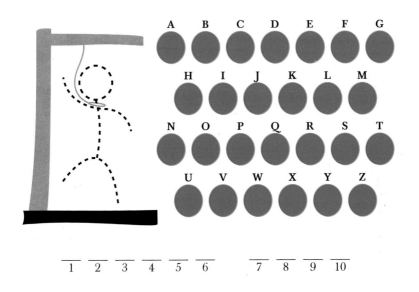

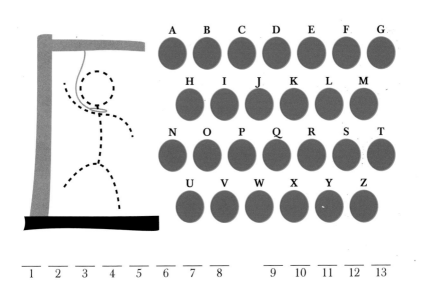

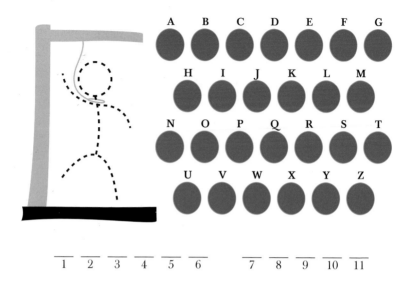

$\overline{}_{1}$ $\overline{}_{2}$ $\overline{}_{3}$ $\overline{}_{4}$ $\overline{}_{5}$ $\overline{}_{6}$ $\overline{}_{7}$ $\overline{}_{8}$ $\overline{}_{9}$ $\overline{}_{10}$ $\overline{}_{11}$

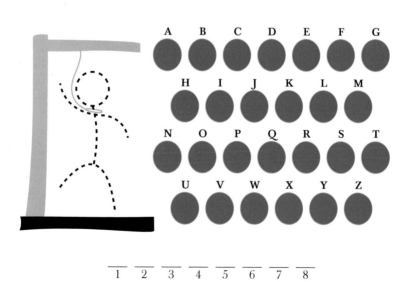

$\overline{}_{1}$ $\overline{}_{2}$ $\overline{}_{3}$ $\overline{}_{4}$ $\overline{}_{5}$ $\overline{}_{6}$ $\overline{}_{7}$ $\overline{}_{8}$

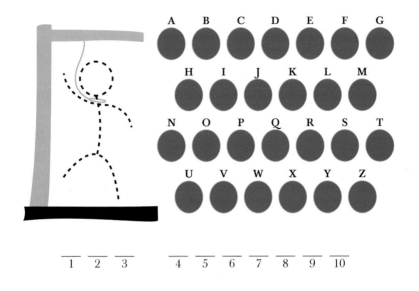

A	B	C	D	E	F	G
H	I	J	K	L	M	
N	O	P	Q	R	S	T
U	V	W	X	Y	Z	

$\overline{\quad}$ $\overline{\quad}$ $\overline{\quad}$ $\overline{\quad}$ $\overline{\quad}$ $\overline{\quad}$ $\overline{\quad}$ $\overline{\quad}$ $\overline{\quad}$ $\overline{\quad}$
  1   2   3   4   5   6   7   8   9   10

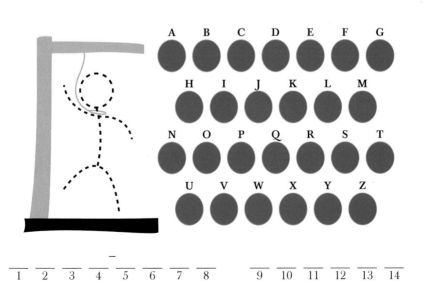

A	B	C	D	E	F	G
H	I	J	K	L	M	
N	O	P	Q	R	S	T
U	V	W	X	Y	Z	

$\overline{\quad}$ $\overline{\quad}$ $\overline{\quad}$ $\overline{\quad}$ $\overline{\quad}$ $\overline{\quad}$ $\overline{\quad}$ $\overline{\quad}$ $\overline{\quad}$ $\overline{\quad}$ $\overline{\quad}$ $\overline{\quad}$ $\overline{\quad}$ $\overline{\quad}$
  1   2   3   4   5   6   7   8   9   10   11   12   13   14

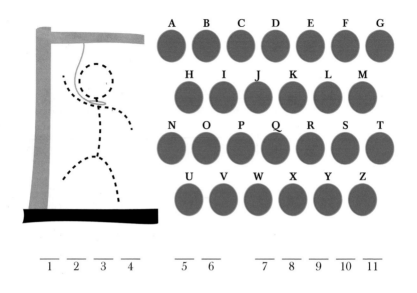

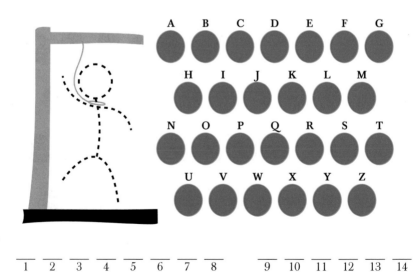

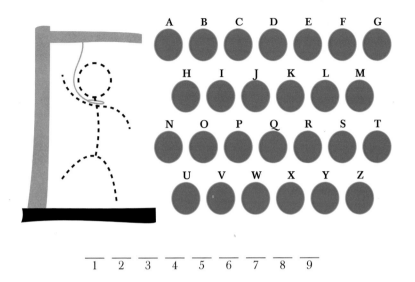

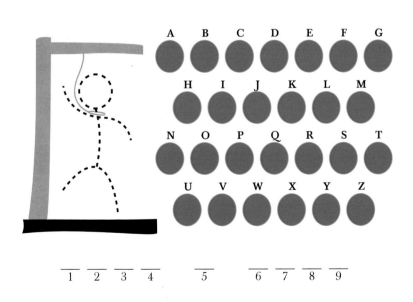

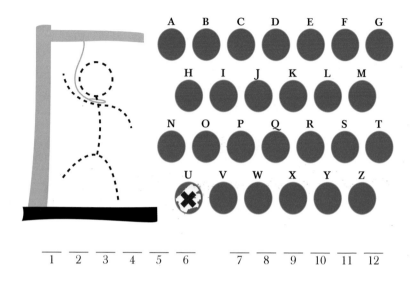

$\overline{}_1$ $\overline{}_2$ $\overline{}_3$ $\overline{}_4$ $\overline{}_5$ $\overline{}_6$ $\quad$ $\overline{}_7$ $\overline{}_8$ $\overline{}_9$ $\overline{}_{10}$ $\overline{}_{11}$ $\overline{}_{12}$

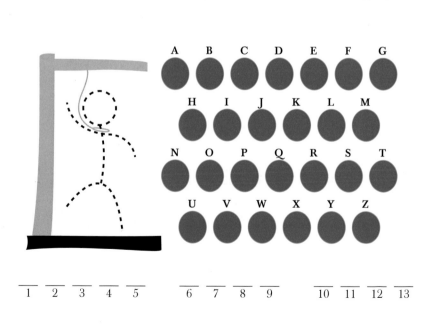

$\overline{}_1$ $\overline{}_2$ $\overline{}_3$ $\overline{}_4$ $\overline{}_5$ $\quad$ $\overline{}_6$ $\overline{}_7$ $\overline{}_8$ $\overline{}_9$ $\quad$ $\overline{}_{10}$ $\overline{}_{11}$ $\overline{}_{12}$ $\overline{}_{13}$

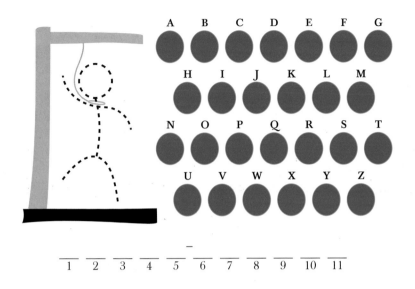

$$\overline{}_1\ \overline{}_2\ \overline{}_3\ \overline{}_4\ \overline{}_5\ \overline{-}_6\ \overline{}_7\ \overline{}_8\ \overline{}_9\ \overline{}_{10}\ \overline{}_{11}$$

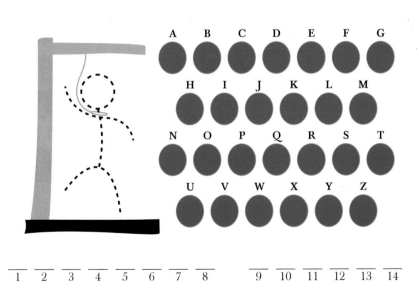

$$\overline{}_1\ \overline{}_2\ \overline{}_3\ \overline{}_4\ \overline{}_5\ \overline{}_6\ \overline{}_7\ \overline{}_8\quad \overline{}_9\ \overline{}_{10}\ \overline{}_{11}\ \overline{}_{12}\ \overline{}_{13}\ \overline{}_{14}$$

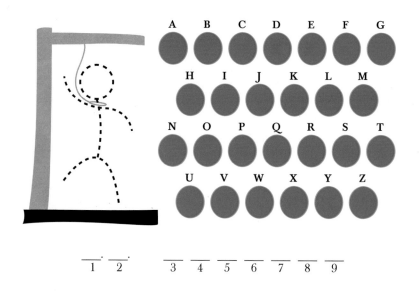

$\overline{}_{1}.\ \overline{}_{2}.\quad \overline{}_{3}\ \overline{}_{4}\ \overline{}_{5}\ \overline{}_{6}\ \overline{}_{7}\ \overline{}_{8}\ \overline{}_{9}$

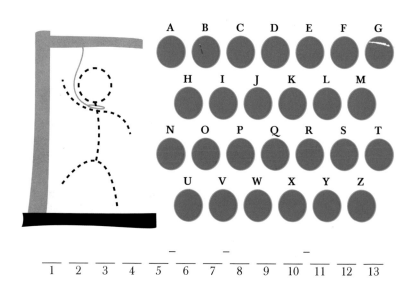

$\overline{}_{1}\ \overline{}_{2}\ \overline{}_{3}\ \overline{}_{4}\ \overline{}_{5}\ \overline{}_{6}\ \overline{}_{7}\ \overline{}_{8}\ \overline{}_{9}\ \overline{}_{10}\ \overline{}_{11}\ \overline{}_{12}\ \overline{}_{13}$

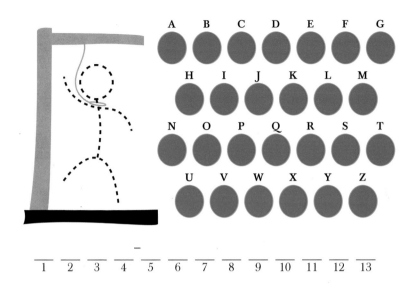

$$\overline{}_{1} \quad \overline{}_{2} \quad \overline{}_{3} \quad \overline{}_{4} \quad \overline{}_{5} \quad \overline{}_{6} \quad \overline{}_{7} \quad \overline{}_{8} \quad \overline{}_{9} \quad \overline{}_{10} \quad \overline{}_{11} \quad \overline{}_{12} \quad \overline{}_{13}$$

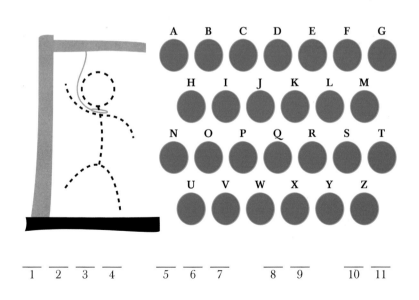

$$\overline{}_{1} \quad \overline{}_{2} \quad \overline{}_{3} \quad \overline{}_{4} \qquad \overline{}_{5} \quad \overline{}_{6} \quad \overline{}_{7} \qquad \overline{}_{8} \quad \overline{}_{9} \qquad \overline{}_{10} \quad \overline{}_{11}$$

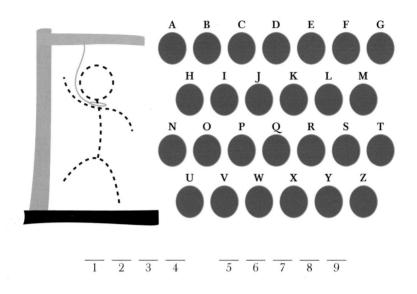

___ ___ ___ ___   ___ ___ ___ ___ ___
 1   2   3   4   5   6   7   8   9

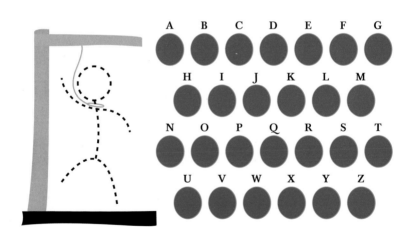

___ ___ ___ ___ ___ ___ ___ ___ ___   ___ ___ ___ ___ ___
 1   2   3   4   5   6   7   8   9   10 11 12 13 14

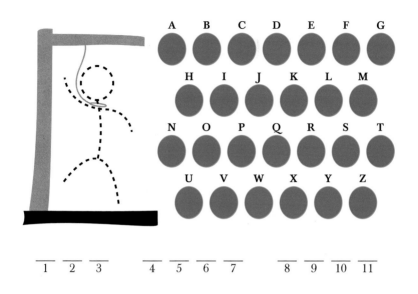

$\overline{1}\ \overline{2}\ \overline{3}\qquad\overline{4}\ \overline{5}\ \overline{6}\ \overline{7}\qquad\overline{8}\ \overline{9}\ \overline{10}\ \overline{11}$

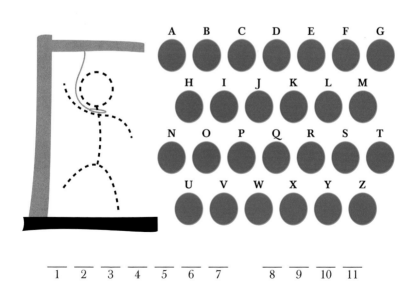

$\overline{1}\ \overline{2}\ \overline{3}\ \overline{4}\ \overline{5}\ \overline{6}\ \overline{7}\qquad\overline{8}\ \overline{9}\ \overline{10}\ \overline{11}$

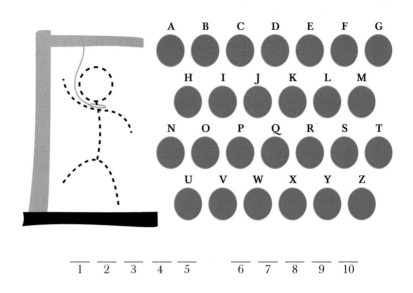

$$\overline{}_1 \ \overline{}_2 \ \overline{}_3 \ \overline{}_4 \ \overline{}_5 \qquad \overline{}_6 \ \overline{}_7 \ \overline{}_8 \ \overline{}_9 \ \overline{}_{10}$$

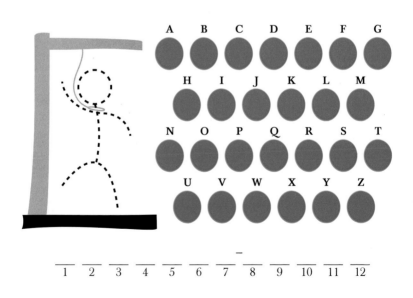

$$\overline{}_1 \ \overline{}_2 \ \overline{}_3 \ \overline{}_4 \ \overline{}_5 \ \overline{}_6 \ \overline{}_7 \ \overline{}_8 \ \overline{}_9 \ \overline{}_{10} \ \overline{}_{11} \ \overline{}_{12}$$

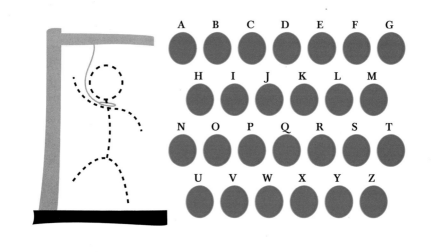

$\overline{}_1$ $\overline{}_2$ $\overline{}_3$ $\overline{}_4$ $\overline{}_5$ $\overline{}_6$ $\overline{}_7$ $\overline{}_8$ $\overline{}_9$ $\overline{}_{10}$ $\overline{}_{11}$ $\overline{}_{12}$ $\overline{}_{13}$ $\overline{}_{14}$

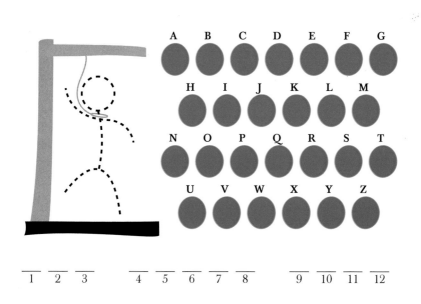

$\overline{}_1$ $\overline{}_2$ $\overline{}_3$ $\overline{}_4$ $\overline{}_5$ $\overline{}_6$ $\overline{}_7$ $\overline{}_8$ $\overline{}_9$ $\overline{}_{10}$ $\overline{}_{11}$ $\overline{}_{12}$

19

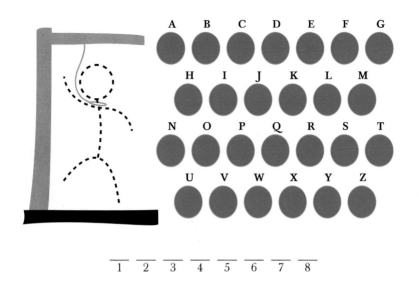

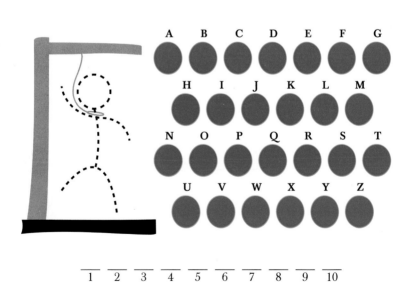

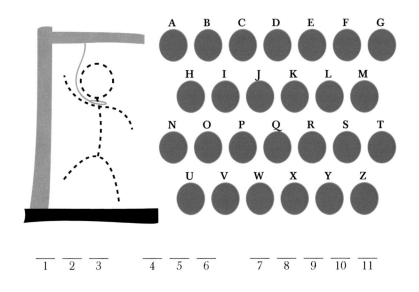

$\overline{}_1$ $\overline{}_2$ $\overline{}_3$ $\overline{}_4$ $\overline{}_5$ $\overline{}_6$ $\overline{}_7$ $\overline{}_8$ $\overline{}_9$ $\overline{}_{10}$ $\overline{}_{11}$

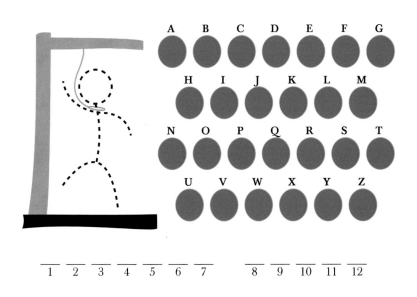

$\overline{}_1$ $\overline{}_2$ $\overline{}_3$ $\overline{}_4$ $\overline{}_5$ $\overline{}_6$ $\overline{}_7$ $\overline{}_8$ $\overline{}_9$ $\overline{}_{10}$ $\overline{}_{11}$ $\overline{}_{12}$

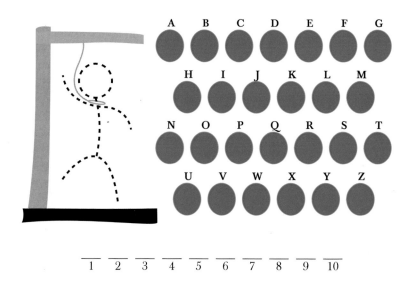

$$\overline{}_1 \ \overline{}_2 \ \overline{}_3 \ \overline{}_4 \ \overline{}_5 \ \overline{}_6 \ \overline{}_7 \ \overline{}_8 \ \overline{}_9 \ \overline{}_{10}$$

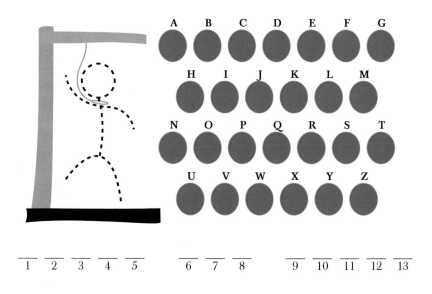

$$\overline{}_1 \ \overline{}_2 \ \overline{}_3 \ \overline{}_4 \ \overline{}_5 \qquad \overline{}_6 \ \overline{}_7 \ \overline{}_8 \qquad \overline{}_9 \ \overline{}_{10} \ \overline{}_{11} \ \overline{}_{12} \ \overline{}_{13}$$

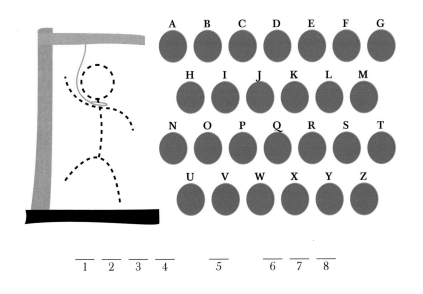

$$\overline{1}\ \overline{2}\ \overline{3}\ \overline{4}\quad \overline{5}\quad \overline{6}\ \overline{7}\ \overline{8}$$

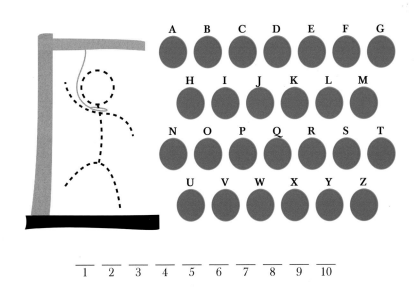

$$\overline{1}\ \overline{2}\ \overline{3}\ \overline{4}\ \overline{5}\ \overline{6}\ \overline{7}\ \overline{8}\ \overline{9}\ \overline{10}$$

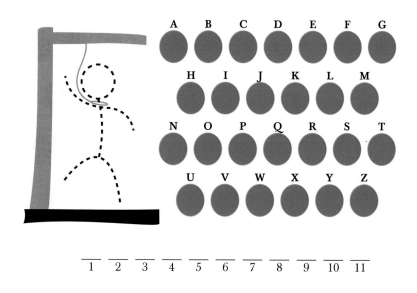

A B C D E F G
H I J K L M
N O P Q R S T
U V W X Y Z

$\overline{1}$ $\overline{2}$ $\overline{3}$ $\overline{4}$ $\overline{5}$ $\overline{6}$ $\overline{7}$ $\overline{8}$ $\overline{9}$ $\overline{10}$ $\overline{11}$

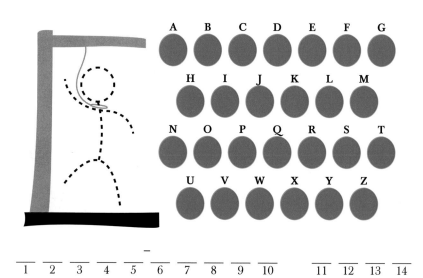

A B C D E F G
H I J K L M
N O P Q R S T
U V W X Y Z

$-$

$\overline{1}$ $\overline{2}$ $\overline{3}$ $\overline{4}$ $\overline{5}$ $\overline{6}$ $\overline{7}$ $\overline{8}$ $\overline{9}$ $\overline{10}$ $\overline{11}$ $\overline{12}$ $\overline{13}$ $\overline{14}$

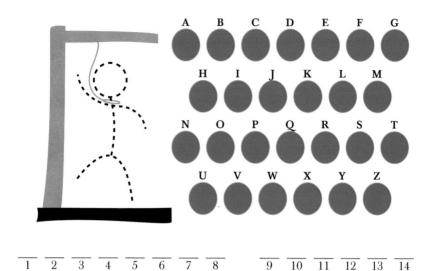

A B C D E F G
H I J K L M
N O P Q R S T
U V W X Y Z

$\overline{1}$ $\overline{2}$ $\overline{3}$ $\overline{4}$ $\overline{5}$ $\overline{6}$ $\overline{7}$ $\overline{8}$ $\overline{9}$ $\overline{10}$ $\overline{11}$ $\overline{12}$ $\overline{13}$ $\overline{14}$

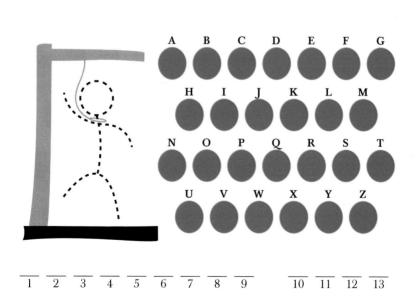

A B C D E F G
H I J K L M
N O P Q R S T
U V W X Y Z

$\overline{1}$ $\overline{2}$ $\overline{3}$ $\overline{4}$ $\overline{5}$ $\overline{6}$ $\overline{7}$ $\overline{8}$ $\overline{9}$ $\overline{10}$ $\overline{11}$ $\overline{12}$ $\overline{13}$

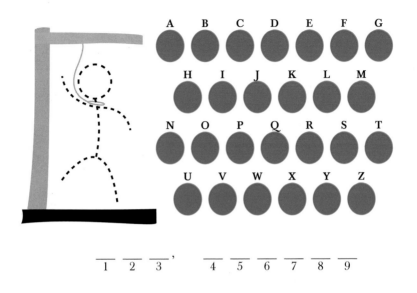

$$\overline{1}\ \overline{2}\ \overline{3}\ ,\quad \overline{4}\ \overline{5}\ \overline{6}\ \overline{7}\ \overline{8}\ \overline{9}$$

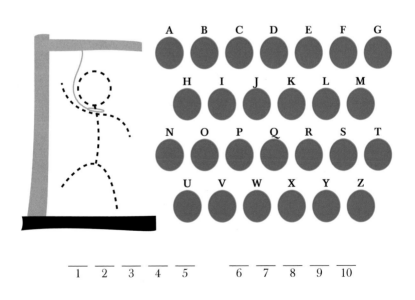

$$\overline{1}\ \overline{2}\ \overline{3}\ \overline{4}\ \overline{5}\quad \overline{6}\ \overline{7}\ \overline{8}\ \overline{9}\ \overline{10}$$

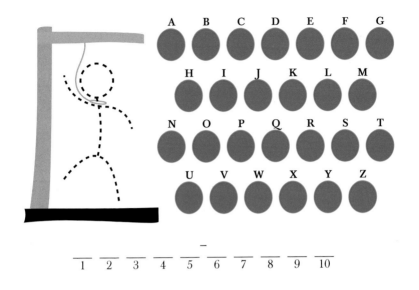

A B C D E F G

H I J K L M

N O P Q R S T

U V W X Y Z

$$\overline{}_{1} \ \overline{}_{2} \ \overline{}_{3} \ \overline{}_{4} \ \overline{}_{5} \ \overline{-}_{6} \ \overline{}_{7} \ \overline{}_{8} \ \overline{}_{9} \ \overline{}_{10}$$

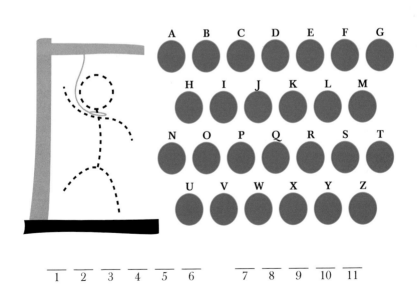

A B C D E F G

H I J K L M

N O P Q R S T

U V W X Y Z

$$\overline{}_{1} \ \overline{}_{2} \ \overline{}_{3} \ \overline{}_{4} \ \overline{}_{5} \ \overline{}_{6} \qquad \overline{}_{7} \ \overline{}_{8} \ \overline{}_{9} \ \overline{}_{10} \ \overline{}_{11}$$

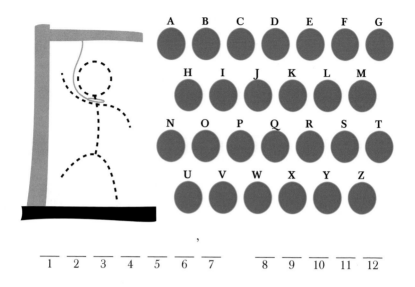

$\overline{\rule{0.7em}{0pt}}_{1}$ $\overline{\rule{0.7em}{0pt}}_{2}$ $\overline{\rule{0.7em}{0pt}}_{3}$ $\overline{\rule{0.7em}{0pt}}_{4}$ $\overline{\rule{0.7em}{0pt}}_{5}$ $\overline{\rule{0.7em}{0pt}}_{6}$ $\overline{\rule{0.7em}{0pt}}_{7}$, $\overline{\rule{0.7em}{0pt}}_{8}$ $\overline{\rule{0.7em}{0pt}}_{9}$ $\overline{\rule{0.7em}{0pt}}_{10}$ $\overline{\rule{0.7em}{0pt}}_{11}$ $\overline{\rule{0.7em}{0pt}}_{12}$

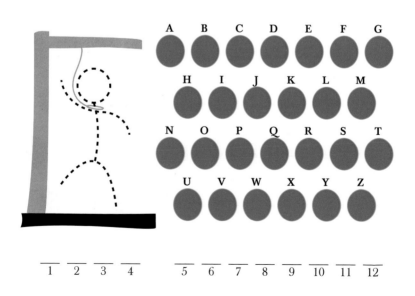

$\overline{\rule{0.7em}{0pt}}_{1}$ $\overline{\rule{0.7em}{0pt}}_{2}$ $\overline{\rule{0.7em}{0pt}}_{3}$ $\overline{\rule{0.7em}{0pt}}_{4}$ $\overline{\rule{0.7em}{0pt}}_{5}$ $\overline{\rule{0.7em}{0pt}}_{6}$ $\overline{\rule{0.7em}{0pt}}_{7}$ $\overline{\rule{0.7em}{0pt}}_{8}$ $\overline{\rule{0.7em}{0pt}}_{9}$ $\overline{\rule{0.7em}{0pt}}_{10}$ $\overline{\rule{0.7em}{0pt}}_{11}$ $\overline{\rule{0.7em}{0pt}}_{12}$

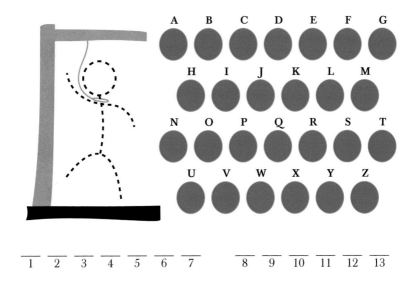

A	B	C	D	E	F	G
H	I	J	K	L	M	
N	O	P	Q	R	S	T
U	V	W	X	Y	Z	

$\overline{1}$ $\overline{2}$ $\overline{3}$ $\overline{4}$ $\overline{5}$ $\overline{6}$ $\overline{7}$ $\overline{8}$ $\overline{9}$ $\overline{10}$ $\overline{11}$ $\overline{12}$ $\overline{13}$

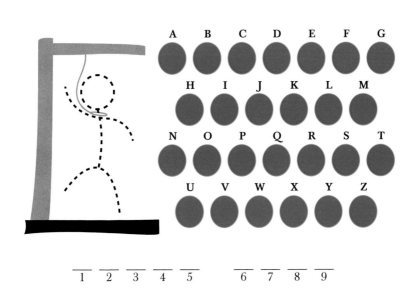

A	B	C	D	E	F	G
H	I	J	K	L	M	
N	O	P	Q	R	S	T
U	V	W	X	Y	Z	

$\overline{1}$ $\overline{2}$ $\overline{3}$ $\overline{4}$ $\overline{5}$ $\overline{6}$ $\overline{7}$ $\overline{8}$ $\overline{9}$

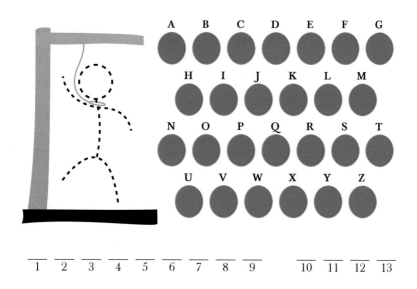

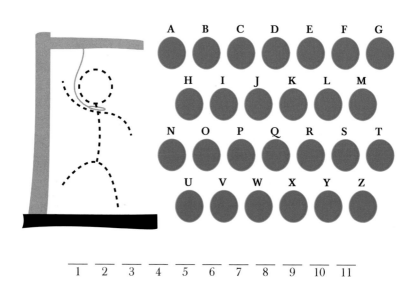

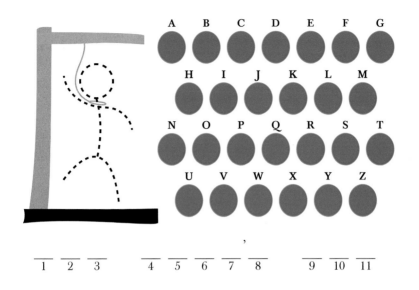

$$\overline{\underset{1}{\quad}} \ \overline{\underset{2}{\quad}} \ \overline{\underset{3}{\quad}} \qquad \overline{\underset{4}{\quad}} \ \overline{\underset{5}{\quad}} \ \overline{\underset{6}{\quad}} \ \overline{\underset{7}{\quad}} \ \overline{\underset{8}{\quad}} , \qquad \overline{\underset{9}{\quad}} \ \overline{\underset{10}{\quad}} \ \overline{\underset{11}{\quad}}$$

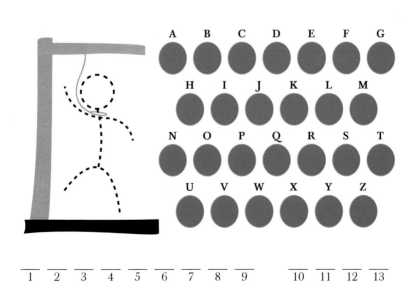

$$\overline{\underset{1}{\quad}} \ \overline{\underset{2}{\quad}} \ \overline{\underset{3}{\quad}} \ \overline{\underset{4}{\quad}} \ \overline{\underset{5}{\quad}} \ \overline{\underset{6}{\quad}} \ \overline{\underset{7}{\quad}} \ \overline{\underset{8}{\quad}} \ \overline{\underset{9}{\quad}} \qquad \overline{\underset{10}{\quad}} \ \overline{\underset{11}{\quad}} \ \overline{\underset{12}{\quad}} \ \overline{\underset{13}{\quad}}$$

31

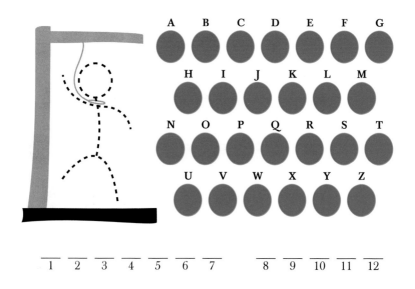

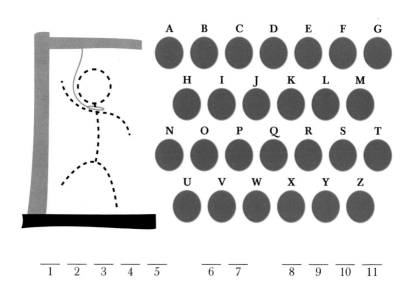

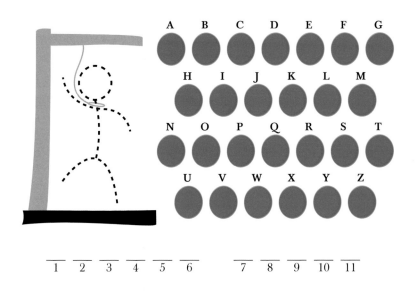

A B C D E F G
H I J K L M
N O P Q R S T
U V W X Y Z

$\overline{}_{1}$ $\overline{}_{2}$ $\overline{}_{3}$ $\overline{}_{4}$ $\overline{}_{5}$ $\overline{}_{6}$ $\overline{}_{7}$ $\overline{}_{8}$ $\overline{}_{9}$ $\overline{}_{10}$ $\overline{}_{11}$

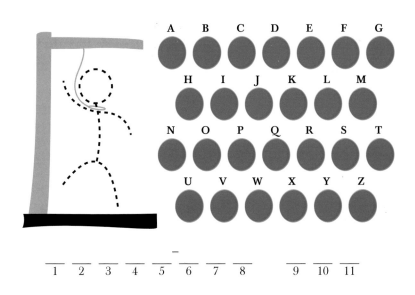

A B C D E F G
H I J K L M
N O P Q R S T
U V W X Y Z

$\overline{}_{1}$ $\overline{}_{2}$ $\overline{}_{3}$ $\overline{}_{4}$ $\overline{}_{5}$ $\overline{}_{6}$ $\overline{}_{7}$ $\overline{}_{8}$ $\overline{}_{9}$ $\overline{}_{10}$ $\overline{}_{11}$

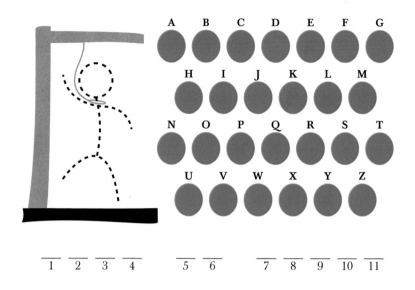

A B C D E F G
H I J K L M
N O P Q R S T
U V W X Y Z

$\overline{\ \ }_{1}\ \overline{\ \ }_{2}\ \overline{\ \ }_{3}\ \overline{\ \ }_{4}\quad \overline{\ \ }_{5}\ \overline{\ \ }_{6}\quad \overline{\ \ }_{7}\ \overline{\ \ }_{8}\ \overline{\ \ }_{9}\ \overline{\ \ }_{10}\ \overline{\ \ }_{11}$

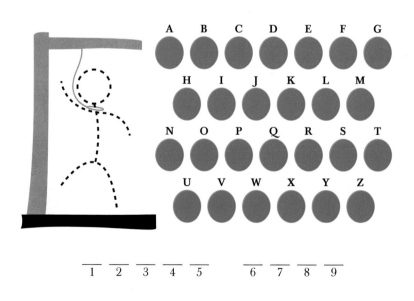

A B C D E F G
H I J K L M
N O P Q R S T
U V W X Y Z

$\overline{\ \ }_{1}\ \overline{\ \ }_{2}\ \overline{\ \ }_{3}\ \overline{\ \ }_{4}\ \overline{\ \ }_{5}\quad \overline{\ \ }_{6}\ \overline{\ \ }_{7}\ \overline{\ \ }_{8}\ \overline{\ \ }_{9}$

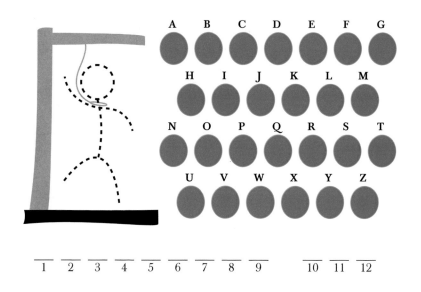

A B C D E F G
H I J K L M
N O P Q R S T
U V W X Y Z

$\overline{1}$ $\overline{2}$ $\overline{3}$ $\overline{4}$ $\overline{5}$ $\overline{6}$ $\overline{7}$ $\overline{8}$ $\overline{9}$ $\overline{10}$ $\overline{11}$ $\overline{12}$

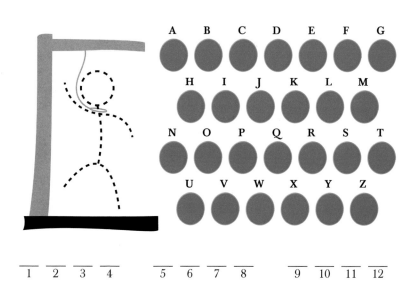

A B C D E F G
H I J K L M
N O P Q R S T
U V W X Y Z

$\overline{1}$ $\overline{2}$ $\overline{3}$ $\overline{4}$ $\overline{5}$ $\overline{6}$ $\overline{7}$ $\overline{8}$ $\overline{9}$ $\overline{10}$ $\overline{11}$ $\overline{12}$

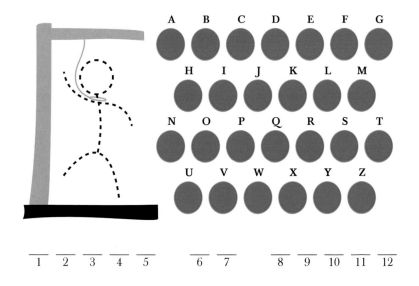

$\overline{1}$ $\overline{2}$ $\overline{3}$ $\overline{4}$ $\overline{5}$ $\overline{6}$ $\overline{7}$ $\overline{8}$ $\overline{9}$ $\overline{10}$ $\overline{11}$ $\overline{12}$

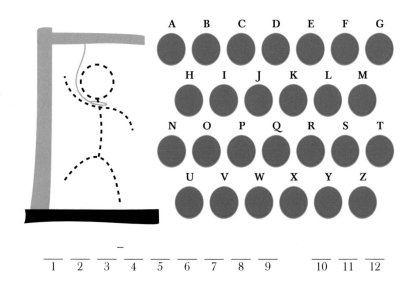

$\overline{1}$ $\overline{2}$ $\overline{3}$ $\overline{4}$ $\overline{5}$ $\overline{6}$ $\overline{7}$ $\overline{8}$ $\overline{9}$ $\overline{10}$ $\overline{11}$ $\overline{12}$

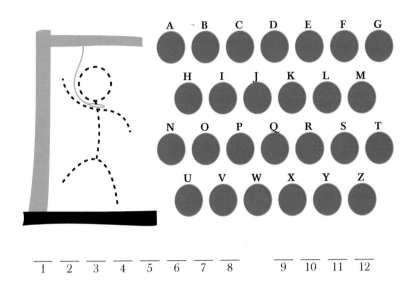

A B C D E F G
H I J K L M
N O P Q R S T
U V W X Y Z

‾1‾ ‾2‾ ‾3‾ ‾4‾ ‾5‾ ‾6‾ ‾7‾ ‾8‾   ‾9‾ ‾10‾ ‾11‾ ‾12‾

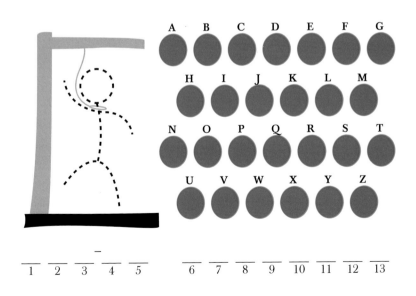

A B C D E F G
H I J K L M
N O P Q R S T
U V W X Y Z

‾1‾ ‾2‾ ‾3‾ ‾4‾ ‾5‾   ‾6‾ ‾7‾ ‾8‾ ‾9‾ ‾10‾ ‾11‾ ‾12‾ ‾13‾

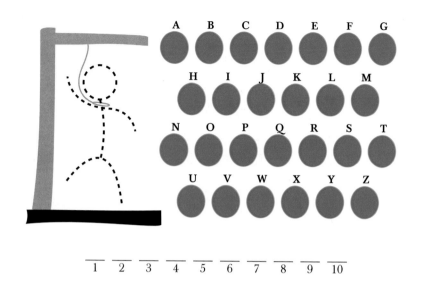

A B C D E F G
H I J K L M
N O P Q R S T
U V W X Y Z

$\overline{1}$ $\overline{2}$ $\overline{3}$ $\overline{4}$ $\overline{5}$ $\overline{6}$ $\overline{7}$ $\overline{8}$ $\overline{9}$ $\overline{10}$

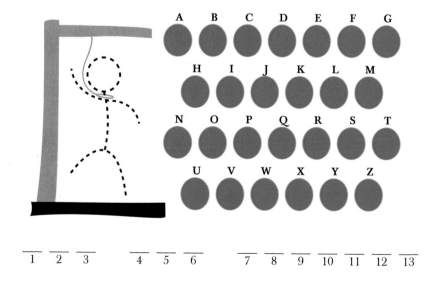

A B C D E F G
H I J K L M
N O P Q R S T
U V W X Y Z

$\overline{1}$ $\overline{2}$ $\overline{3}$ $\overline{4}$ $\overline{5}$ $\overline{6}$ $\overline{7}$ $\overline{8}$ $\overline{9}$ $\overline{10}$ $\overline{11}$ $\overline{12}$ $\overline{13}$

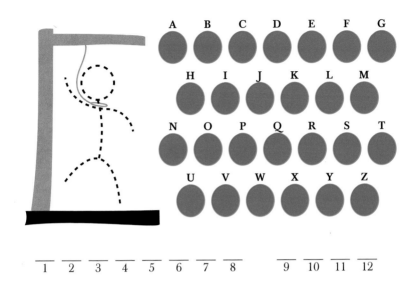

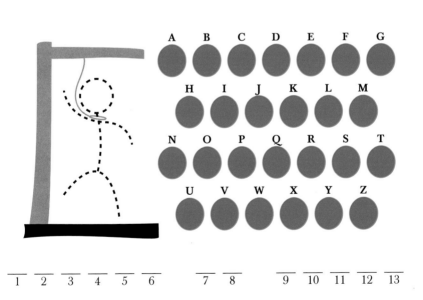

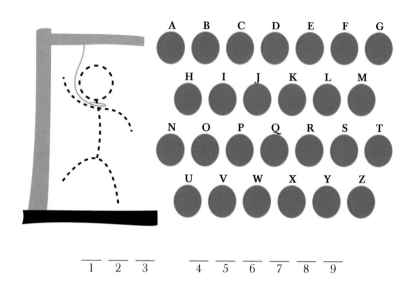

$$\overline{1} \quad \overline{2} \quad \overline{3} \qquad \overline{4} \quad \overline{5} \quad \overline{6} \quad \overline{7} \quad \overline{8} \quad \overline{9}$$

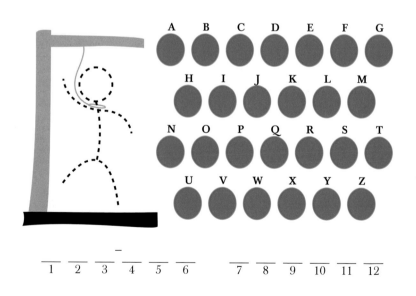

$$\overline{1} \quad \overline{2} \quad \overset{-}{\overline{3}} \quad \overline{4} \quad \overline{5} \quad \overline{6} \qquad \overline{7} \quad \overline{8} \quad \overline{9} \quad \overline{10} \quad \overline{11} \quad \overline{12}$$

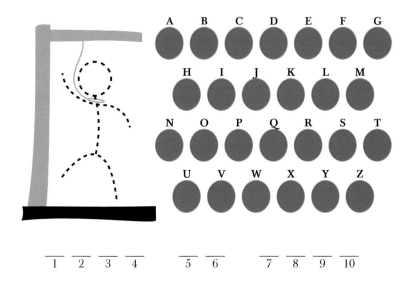

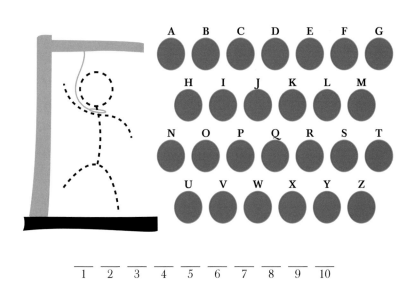

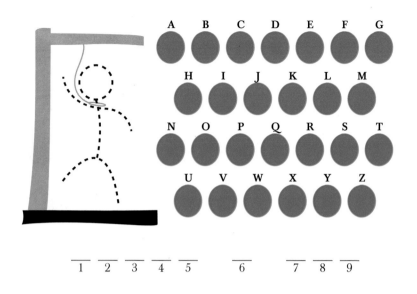

A B C D E F G
H I J K L M
N O P Q R S T
U V W X Y Z

—1— —2— —3— —4— —5— —6— —7— —8— —9—

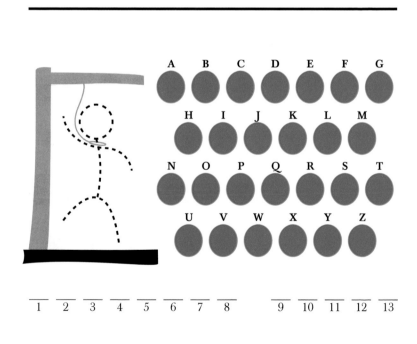

A B C D E F G
H I J K L M
N O P Q R S T
U V W X Y Z

—1— —2— —3— —4— —5— —6— —7— —8— —9— —10— —11— —12— —13—

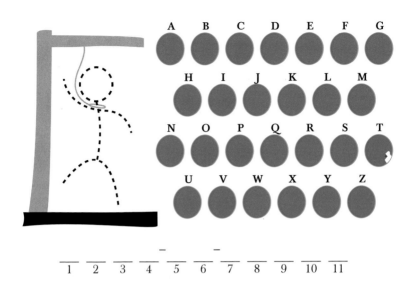

A	B	C	D	E	F	G
H	I	J	K	L	M	
N	O	P	Q	R	S	T
U	V	W	X	Y	Z	

$$\overline{}_{1} \; \overline{}_{2} \; \overline{}_{3} \; \overline{}_{4} \; \overline{\underline{}}_{5} \; \overline{}_{6} \; \overline{\underline{}}_{7} \; \overline{}_{8} \; \overline{}_{9} \; \overline{}_{10} \; \overline{}_{11}$$

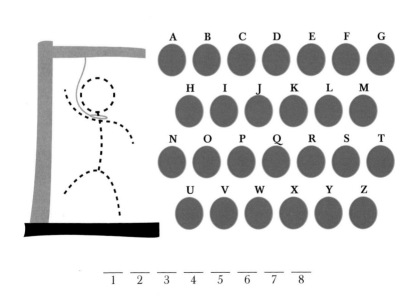

A	B	C	D	E	F	G
H	I	J	K	L	M	
N	O	P	Q	R	S	T
U	V	W	X	Y	Z	

$$\overline{}_{1} \; \overline{}_{2} \; \overline{}_{3} \; \overline{}_{4} \; \overline{}_{5} \; \overline{}_{6} \; \overline{}_{7} \; \overline{}_{8}$$

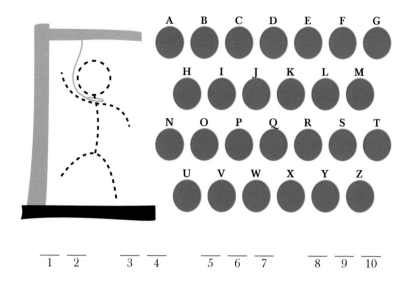

A B C D E F G

H I J K L M

N O P Q R S T

U V W X Y Z

___ ___   ___ ___   ___ ___ ___   ___ ___ ___
 1   2   3   4   5   6   7   8   9   10

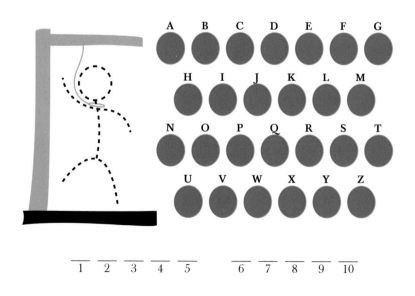

A B C D E F G

H I J K L M

N O P Q R S T

U V W X Y Z

___ ___ ___ ___ ___   ___ ___ ___ ___ ___
 1   2   3   4   5   6   7   8   9   10

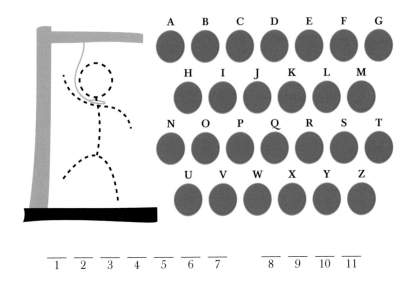

A B C D E F G
H I J K L M
N O P Q R S T
U V W X Y Z

$\overline{}_1$ $\overline{}_2$ $\overline{}_3$ $\overline{}_4$ $\overline{}_5$ $\overline{}_6$ $\overline{}_7$ $\overline{}_8$ $\overline{}_9$ $\overline{}_{10}$ $\overline{}_{11}$

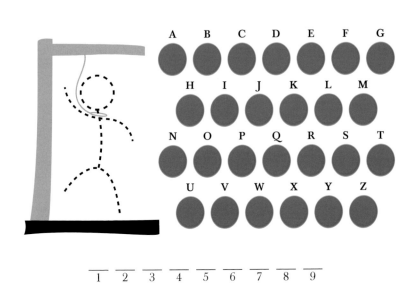

A B C D E F G
H I J K L M
N O P Q R S T
U V W X Y Z

$\overline{}_1$ $\overline{}_2$ $\overline{}_3$ $\overline{}_4$ $\overline{}_5$ $\overline{}_6$ $\overline{}_7$ $\overline{}_8$ $\overline{}_9$

45

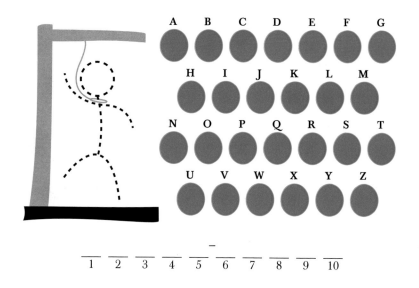

A	B	C	D	E	F	G
H	I	J	K	L	M	
N	O	P	Q	R	S	T
U	V	W	X	Y	Z	

$$\overline{}_1 \quad \overline{}_2 \quad \overline{}_3 \quad \overline{}_4 \quad \overline{}_5 \quad \overline{}_6 \quad \overline{}_7 \quad \overline{}_8 \quad \overline{}_9 \quad \overline{}_{10}$$

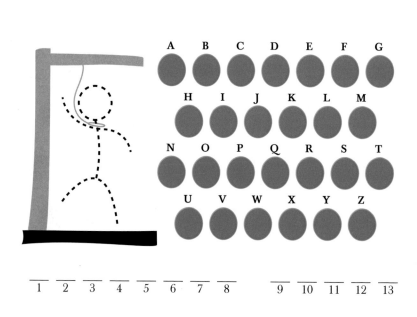

$$\overline{}_1 \quad \overline{}_2 \quad \overline{}_3 \quad \overline{}_4 \quad \overline{}_5 \quad \overline{}_6 \quad \overline{}_7 \quad \overline{}_8 \qquad \overline{}_9 \quad \overline{}_{10} \quad \overline{}_{11} \quad \overline{}_{12} \quad \overline{}_{13}$$

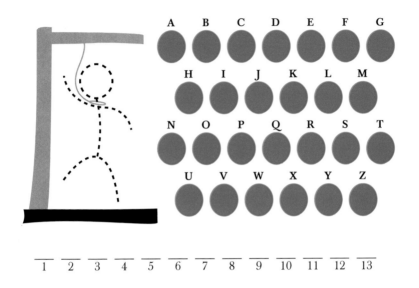

A B C D E F G
H I J K L M
N O P Q R S T
U V W X Y Z

1 2 3 4 5 6 7 8 9 10 11 12 13

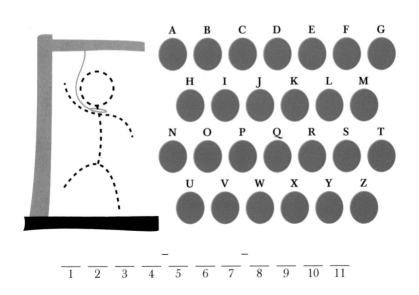

A B C D E F G
H I J K L M
N O P Q R S T
U V W X Y Z

1 2 3 4 — 5 6 7 — 8 9 10 11

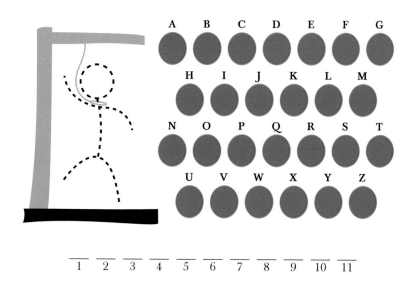

A B C D E F G
H I J K L M
N O P Q R S T
U V W X Y Z

‾1‾ ‾2‾ ‾3‾ ‾4‾ ‾5‾ ‾6‾ ‾7‾ ‾8‾ ‾9‾ ‾10‾ ‾11‾

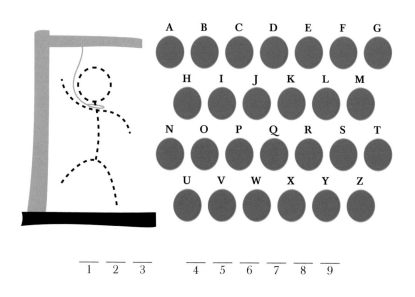

A B C D E F G
H I J K L M
N O P Q R S T
U V W X Y Z

‾1‾ ‾2‾ ‾3‾   ‾4‾ ‾5‾ ‾6‾ ‾7‾ ‾8‾ ‾9‾

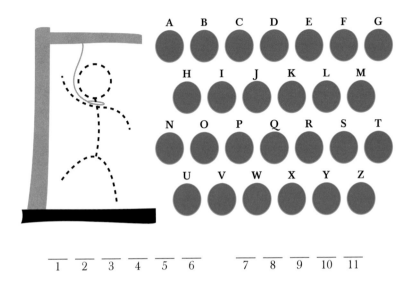

A B C D E F G
H I J K L M
N O P Q R S T
U V W X Y Z

_1_ _2_ _3_ _4_ _5_ _6_   _7_ _8_ _9_ _10_ _11_

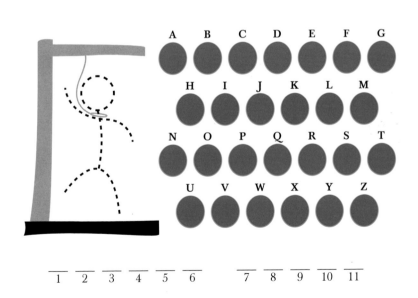

A B C D E F G
H I J K L M
N O P Q R S T
U V W X Y Z

_1_ _2_ _3_ _4_ _5_ _6_   _7_ _8_ _9_ _10_ _11_

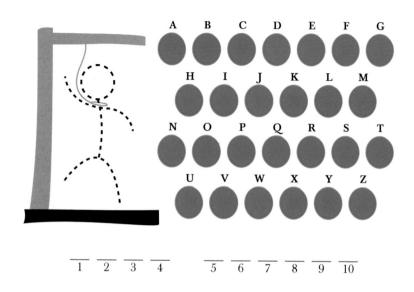

$$\overline{1} \quad \overline{2} \quad \overline{3} \quad \overline{4} \qquad \overline{5} \quad \overline{6} \quad \overline{7} \quad \overline{8} \quad \overline{9} \quad \overline{10}$$

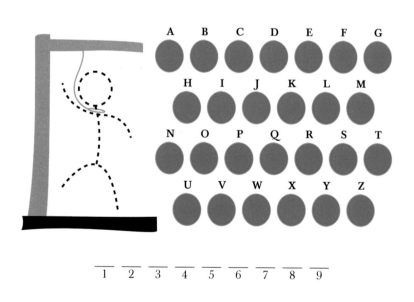

$$\overline{1} \quad \overline{2} \quad \overline{3} \quad \overline{4} \quad \overline{5} \quad \overline{6} \quad \overline{7} \quad \overline{8} \quad \overline{9}$$

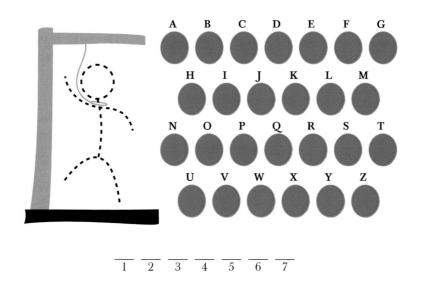

A B C D E F G
H I J K L M
N O P Q R S T
U V W X Y Z

___ ___ ___ ___ ___ ___ ___
 1   2   3   4   5   6   7

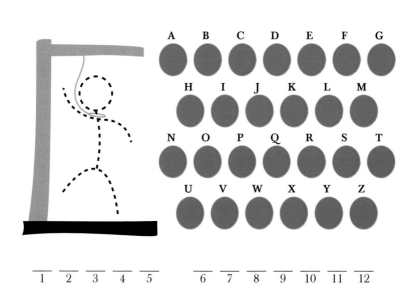

A B C D E F G
H I J K L M
N O P Q R S T
U V W X Y Z

___ ___ ___ ___ ___   ___ ___ ___ ___ ___ ___ ___
 1   2   3   4   5   6   7   8   9   10   11   12

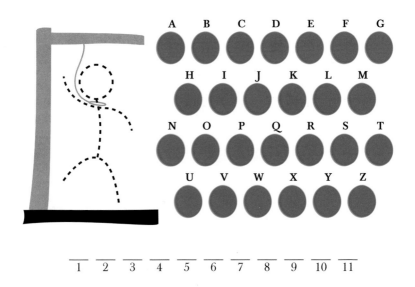

$$\overline{}_{1} \; \overline{}_{2} \; \overline{}_{3} \; \overline{}_{4} \; \overline{}_{5} \; \overline{}_{6} \; \overline{}_{7} \; \overline{}_{8} \; \overline{}_{9} \; \overline{}_{10} \; \overline{}_{11}$$

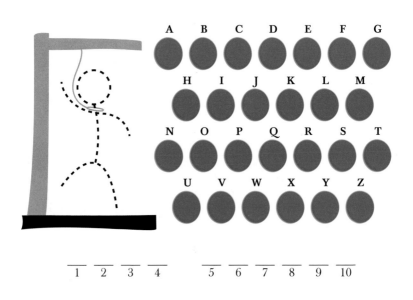

$$\overline{}_{1} \; \overline{}_{2} \; \overline{}_{3} \; \overline{}_{4} \qquad \overline{}_{5} \; \overline{}_{6} \; \overline{}_{7} \; \overline{}_{8} \; \overline{}_{9} \; \overline{}_{10}$$

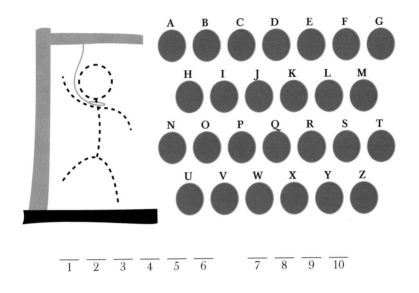

A B C D E F G
H I J K L M
N O P Q R S T
U V W X Y Z

___ ___ ___ ___ ___ ___   ___ ___ ___ ___
 1   2   3   4   5   6   7   8   9   10

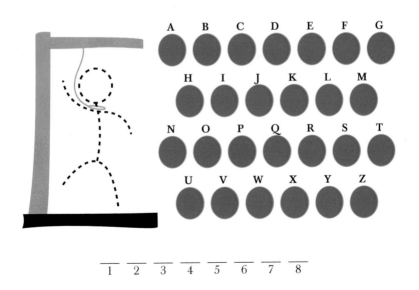

A B C D E F G
H I J K L M
N O P Q R S T
U V W X Y Z

___ ___ ___ ___ ___ ___ ___ ___
 1   2   3   4   5   6   7   8

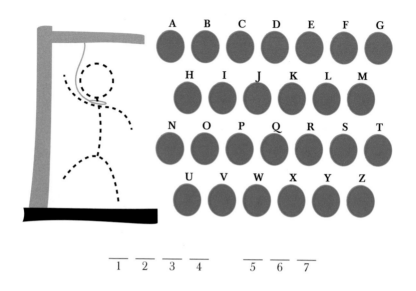

A B C D E F G
H I J K L M
N O P Q R S T
U V W X Y Z

$\overline{}$ $\overline{}$ $\overline{}$ $\overline{}$ $\overline{}$ $\overline{}$ $\overline{}$
1   2   3   4   5   6   7

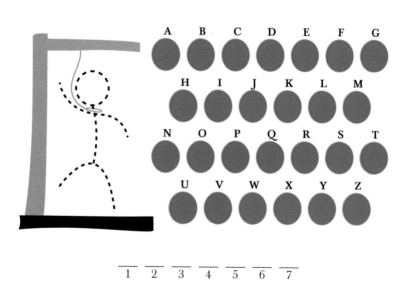

A B C D E F G
H I J K L M
N O P Q R S T
U V W X Y Z

$\overline{}$ $\overline{}$ $\overline{}$ $\overline{}$ $\overline{}$ $\overline{}$ $\overline{}$
1   2   3   4   5   6   7

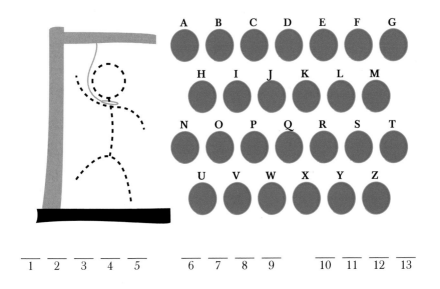

$\overline{1}$ $\overline{2}$ $\overline{3}$ $\overline{4}$ $\overline{5}$ $\quad$ $\overline{6}$ $\overline{7}$ $\overline{8}$ $\overline{9}$ $\quad$ $\overline{10}$ $\overline{11}$ $\overline{12}$ $\overline{13}$

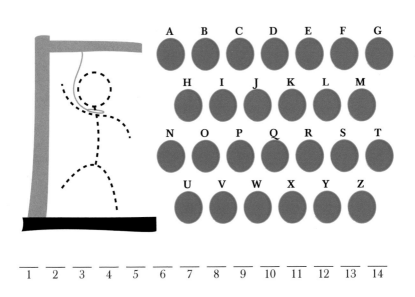

$\overline{1}$ $\overline{2}$ $\overline{3}$ $\overline{4}$ $\overline{5}$ $\overline{6}$ $\overline{7}$ $\overline{8}$ $\overline{9}$ $\overline{10}$ $\overline{11}$ $\overline{12}$ $\overline{13}$ $\overline{14}$

55

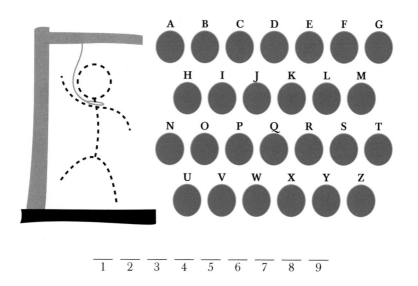

$\overline{}$ $\overline{}$ $\overline{}$ $\overline{}$ $\overline{}$ $\overline{}$ $\overline{}$ $\overline{}$ $\overline{}$
1 2 3 4 5 6 7 8 9

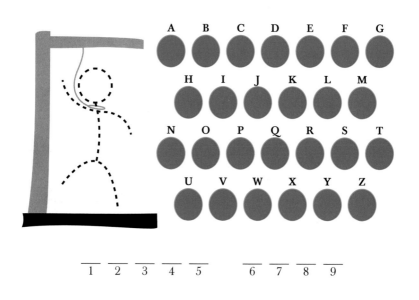

$\overline{}$ $\overline{}$ $\overline{}$ $\overline{}$ $\overline{}$ $\quad$ $\overline{}$ $\overline{}$ $\overline{}$ $\overline{}$
1 2 3 4 5 6 7 8 9

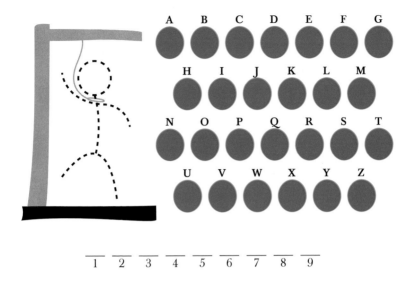

A B C D E F G
H I J K L M
N O P Q R S T
U V W X Y Z

‾1‾ ‾2‾ ‾3‾ ‾4‾ ‾5‾ ‾6‾ ‾7‾ ‾8‾ ‾9‾

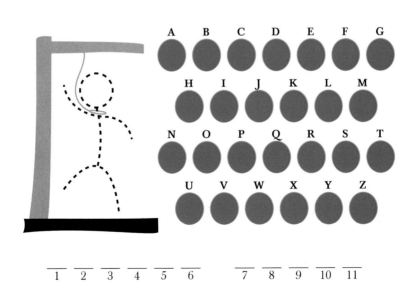

A B C D E F G
H I J K L M
N O P Q R S T
U V W X Y Z

‾1‾ ‾2‾ ‾3‾ ‾4‾ ‾5‾ ‾6‾   ‾7‾ ‾8‾ ‾9‾ ‾10‾ ‾11‾

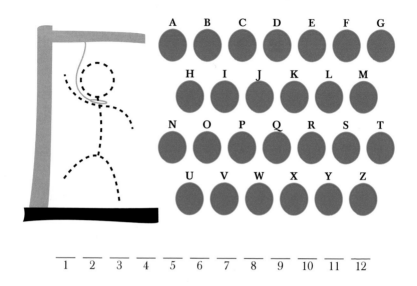

A B C D E F G
H I J K L M
N O P Q R S T
U V W X Y Z

$\overline{1}$ $\overline{2}$ $\overline{3}$ $\overline{4}$ $\overline{5}$ $\overline{6}$ $\overline{7}$ $\overline{8}$ $\overline{9}$ $\overline{10}$ $\overline{11}$ $\overline{12}$

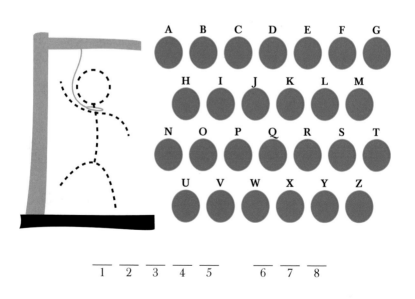

A B C D E F G
H I J K L M
N O P Q R S T
U V W X Y Z

$\overline{1}$ $\overline{2}$ $\overline{3}$ $\overline{4}$ $\overline{5}$ $\overline{6}$ $\overline{7}$ $\overline{8}$

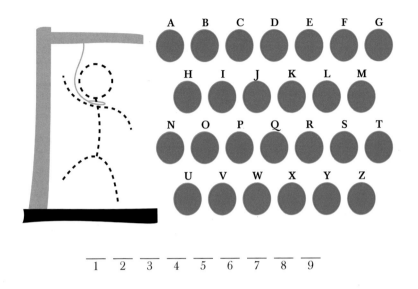

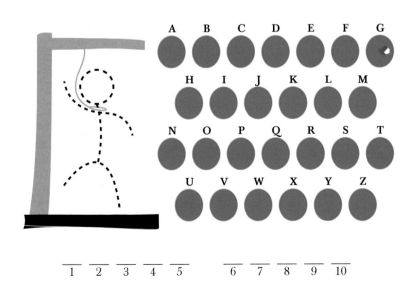

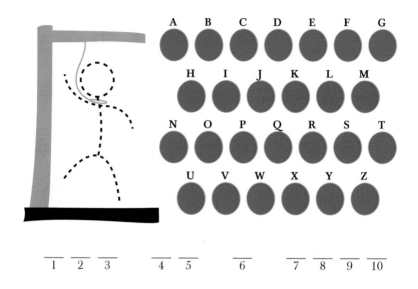

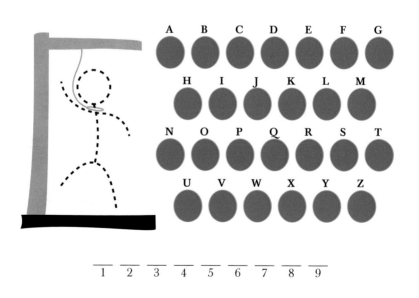

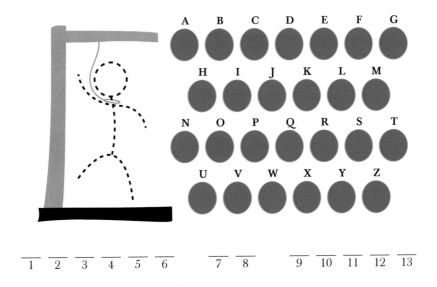

A B C D E F G
H I J K L M
N O P Q R S T
U V W X Y Z

‾1‾ ‾2‾ ‾3‾ ‾4‾ ‾5‾ ‾6‾ ‾7‾ ‾8‾ ‾9‾ ‾10‾ ‾11‾ ‾12‾ ‾13‾

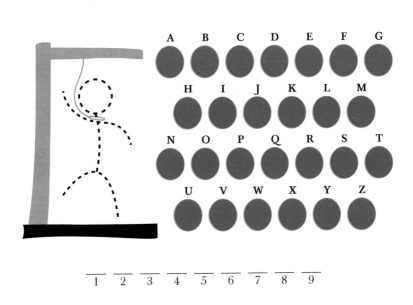

A B C D E F G
H I J K L M
N O P Q R S T
U V W X Y Z

‾1‾ ‾2‾ ‾3‾ ‾4‾ ‾5‾ ‾6‾ ‾7‾ ‾8‾ ‾9‾

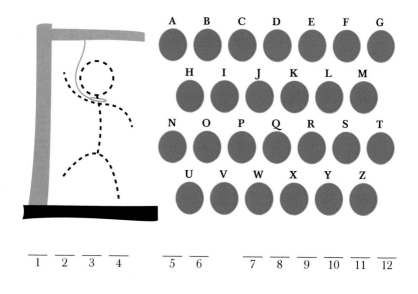

A B C D E F G
H I J K L M
N O P Q R S T
U V W X Y Z

$\overline{\;\;}$ $\overline{\;\;}$ $\overline{\;\;}$ $\overline{\;\;}$ $\overline{\;\;}$ $\overline{\;\;}$ $\overline{\;\;}$ $\overline{\;\;}$ $\overline{\;\;}$ $\overline{\;\;}$ $\overline{\;\;}$ $\overline{\;\;}$
1 2 3 4   5 6   7 8 9 10 11 12

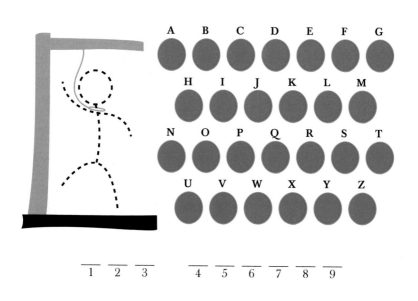

A B C D E F G
H I J K L M
N O P Q R S T
U V W X Y Z

$\overline{\;\;}$ $\overline{\;\;}$ $\overline{\;\;}$ $\overline{\;\;}$ $\overline{\;\;}$ $\overline{\;\;}$ $\overline{\;\;}$ $\overline{\;\;}$ $\overline{\;\;}$
1 2 3   4 5 6 7 8 9

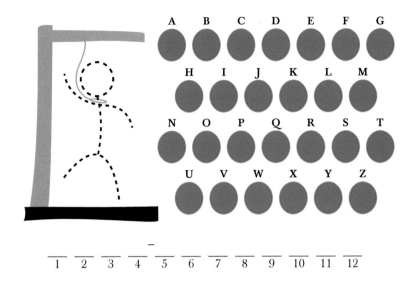

$\overline{}_1$ $\overline{}_2$ $\overline{}_3$ $\overline{}_4$ $\overline{}_5$ $\overline{}_6$ $\overline{}_7$ $\overline{}_8$ $\overline{}_9$ $\overline{}_{10}$ $\overline{}_{11}$ $\overline{}_{12}$

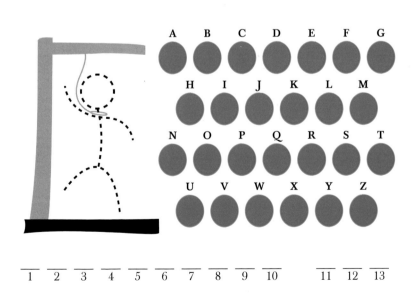

$\overline{}_1$ $\overline{}_2$ $\overline{}_3$ $\overline{}_4$ $\overline{}_5$ $\overline{}_6$ $\overline{}_7$ $\overline{}_8$ $\overline{}_9$ $\overline{}_{10}$ $\overline{}_{11}$ $\overline{}_{12}$ $\overline{}_{13}$

63

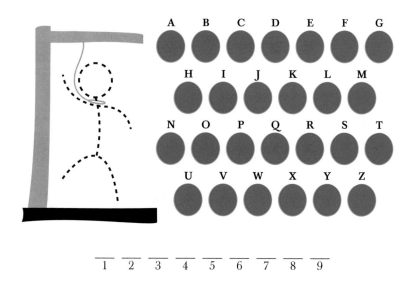

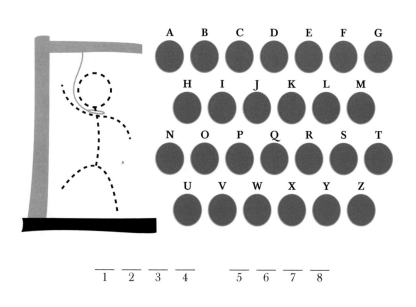

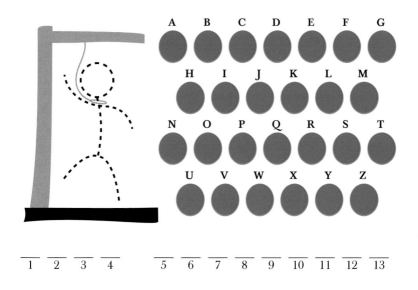

A B C D E F G

H I J K L M

N O P Q R S T

U V W X Y Z

$\overline{1}$ $\overline{2}$ $\overline{3}$ $\overline{4}$ $\overline{5}$ $\overline{6}$ $\overline{7}$ $\overline{8}$ $\overline{9}$ $\overline{10}$ $\overline{11}$ $\overline{12}$ $\overline{13}$

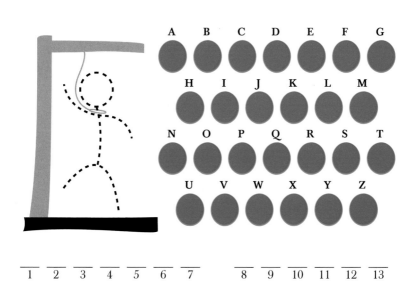

A B C D E F G

H I J K L M

N O P Q R S T

U V W X Y Z

$\overline{1}$ $\overline{2}$ $\overline{3}$ $\overline{4}$ $\overline{5}$ $\overline{6}$ $\overline{7}$ $\overline{8}$ $\overline{9}$ $\overline{10}$ $\overline{11}$ $\overline{12}$ $\overline{13}$

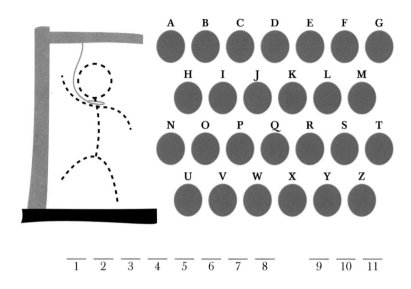

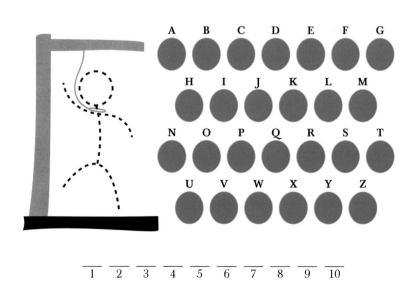

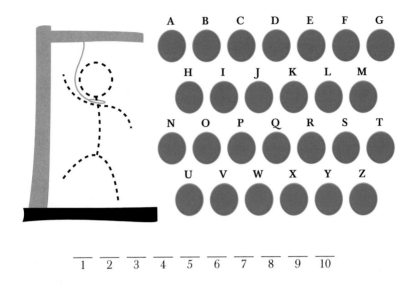

A B C D E F G
H I J K L M
N O P Q R S T
U V W X Y Z

$\overline{1}$ $\overline{2}$ $\overline{3}$ $\overline{4}$ $\overline{5}$ $\overline{6}$ $\overline{7}$ $\overline{8}$ $\overline{9}$ $\overline{10}$

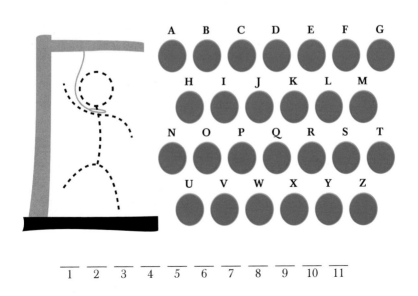

A B C D E F G
H I J K L M
N O P Q R S T
U V W X Y Z

$\overline{1}$ $\overline{2}$ $\overline{3}$ $\overline{4}$ $\overline{5}$ $\overline{6}$ $\overline{7}$ $\overline{8}$ $\overline{9}$ $\overline{10}$ $\overline{11}$

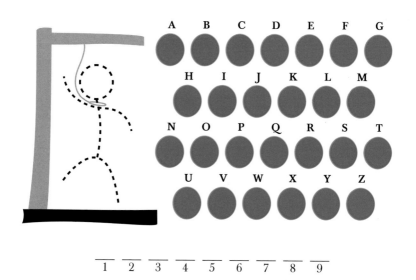

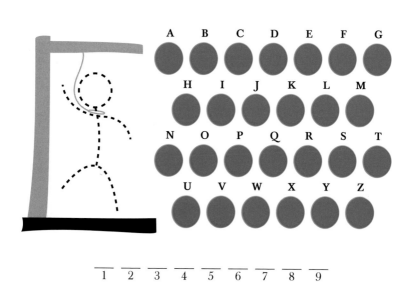

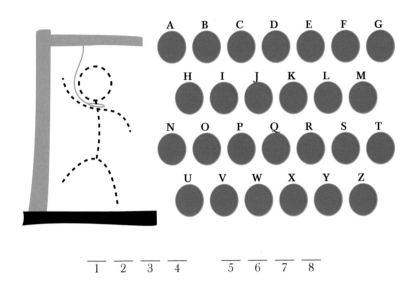

A B C D E F G
H I J K L M
N O P Q R S T
U V W X Y Z

‾1‾ ‾2‾ ‾3‾ ‾4‾   ‾5‾ ‾6‾ ‾7‾ ‾8‾

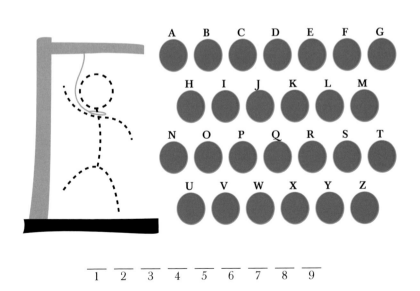

A B C D E F G
H I J K L M
N O P Q R S T
U V W X Y Z

‾1‾ ‾2‾ ‾3‾ ‾4‾ ‾5‾ ‾6‾ ‾7‾ ‾8‾ ‾9‾

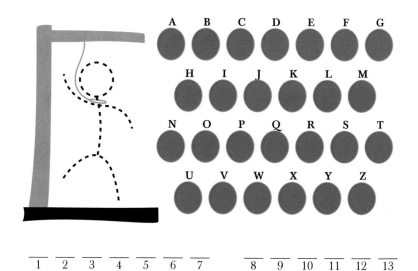

A B C D E F G
H I J K L M
N O P Q R S T
U V W X Y Z

$\overline{1}$ $\overline{2}$ $\overline{3}$ $\overline{4}$ $\overline{5}$ $\overline{6}$ $\overline{7}$ $\overline{8}$ $\overline{9}$ $\overline{10}$ $\overline{11}$ $\overline{12}$ $\overline{13}$

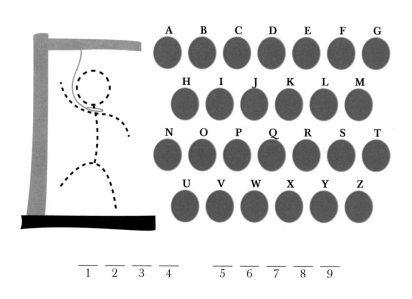

A B C D E F G
H I J K L M
N O P Q R S T
U V W X Y Z

$\overline{1}$ $\overline{2}$ $\overline{3}$ $\overline{4}$ $\overline{5}$ $\overline{6}$ $\overline{7}$ $\overline{8}$ $\overline{9}$

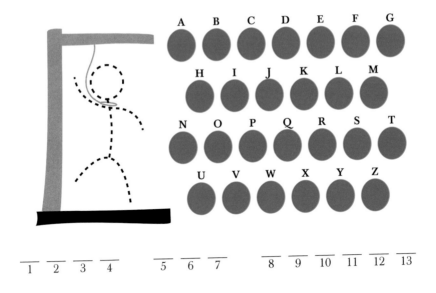

$\overline{}_1$ $\overline{}_2$ $\overline{}_3$ $\overline{}_4$ $\quad$ $\overline{}_5$ $\overline{}_6$ $\overline{}_7$ $\quad$ $\overline{}_8$ $\overline{}_9$ $\overline{}_{10}$ $\overline{}_{11}$ $\overline{}_{12}$ $\overline{}_{13}$

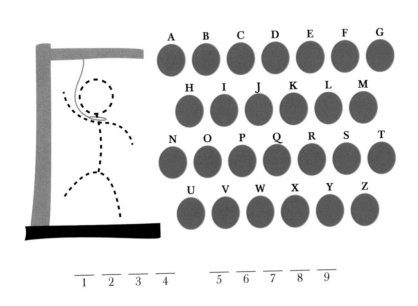

$\overline{}_1$ $\overline{}_2$ $\overline{}_3$ $\overline{}_4$ $\quad$ $\overline{}_5$ $\overline{}_6$ $\overline{}_7$ $\overline{}_8$ $\overline{}_9$

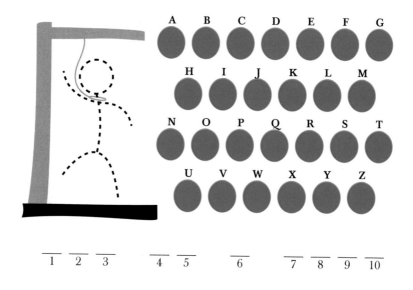

$\overline{}_{1}\ \overline{}_{2}\ \overline{}_{3}\quad \overline{}_{4}\ \overline{}_{5}\quad \overline{}_{6}\quad \overline{}_{7}\ \overline{}_{8}\ \overline{}_{9}\ \overline{}_{10}$

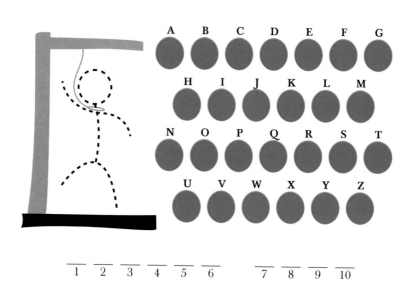

$\overline{}_{1}\ \overline{}_{2}\ \overline{}_{3}\ \overline{}_{4}\ \overline{}_{5}\ \overline{}_{6}\quad \overline{}_{7}\ \overline{}_{8}\ \overline{}_{9}\ \overline{}_{10}$

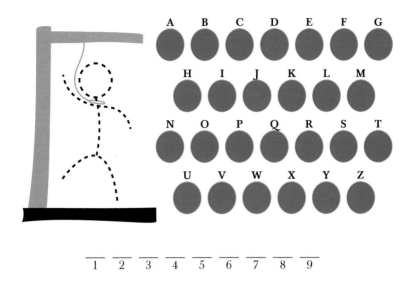

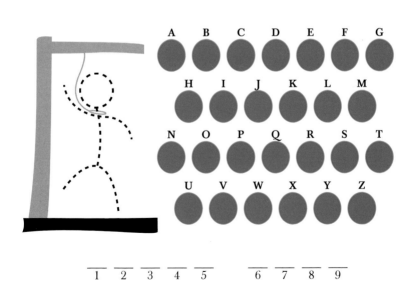

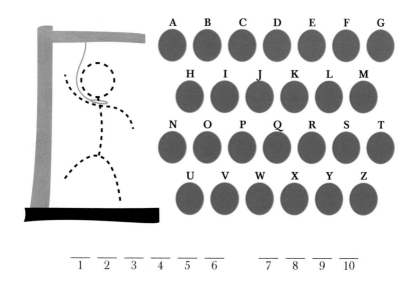

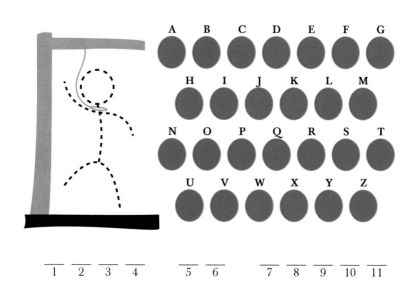

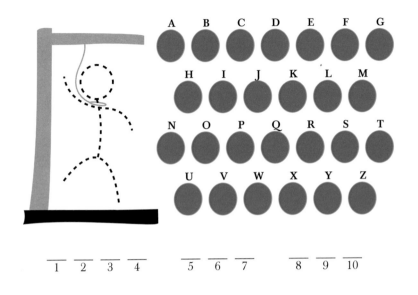

A B C D E F G
H I J K L M
N O P Q R S T
U V W X Y Z

$\overline{}_{1}$ $\overline{}_{2}$ $\overline{}_{3}$ $\overline{}_{4}$ $\overline{}_{5}$ $\overline{}_{6}$ $\overline{}_{7}$ $\overline{}_{8}$ $\overline{}_{9}$ $\overline{}_{10}$

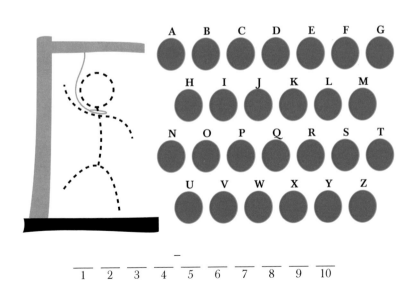

A B C D E F G
H I J K L M
N O P Q R S T
U V W X Y Z

$\overline{}_{1}$ $\overline{}_{2}$ $\overline{}_{3}$ $\overline{}_{4}$ $\overline{}_{5}$ $\overline{}_{6}$ $\overline{}_{7}$ $\overline{}_{8}$ $\overline{}_{9}$ $\overline{}_{10}$

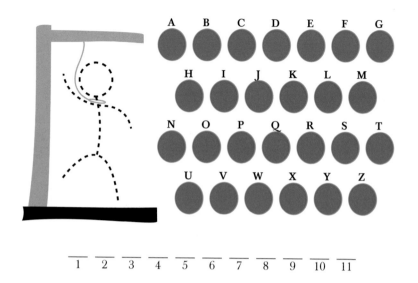

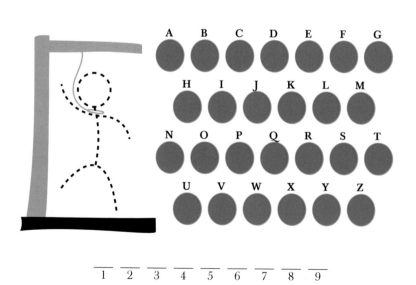

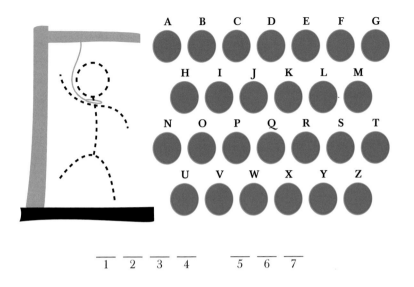

A B C D E F G

H I J K L M

N O P Q R S T

U V W X Y Z

—1— —2— —3— —4—   —5— —6— —7—

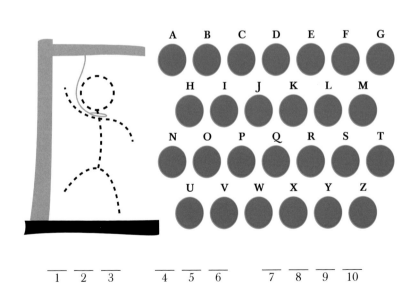

A B C D E F G

H I J K L M

N O P Q R S T

U V W X Y Z

—1— —2— —3—   —4— —5— —6—   —7— —8— —9— —10—

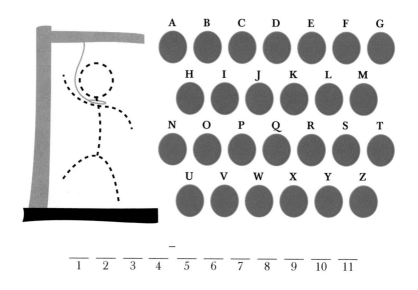

A B C D E F G
H I J K L M
N O P Q R S T
U V W X Y Z

$\overline{1}$ $\overline{2}$ $\overline{3}$ $\overline{4}$ $\overline{5}$ $\overline{6}$ $\overline{7}$ $\overline{8}$ $\overline{9}$ $\overline{10}$ $\overline{11}$

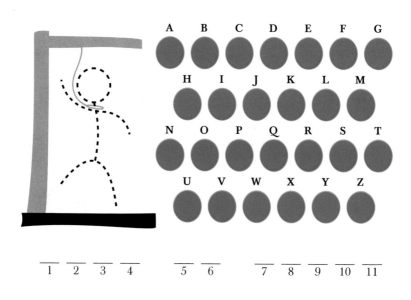

A B C D E F G
H I J K L M
N O P Q R S T
U V W X Y Z

$\overline{1}$ $\overline{2}$ $\overline{3}$ $\overline{4}$ $\overline{5}$ $\overline{6}$ $\overline{7}$ $\overline{8}$ $\overline{9}$ $\overline{10}$ $\overline{11}$

78

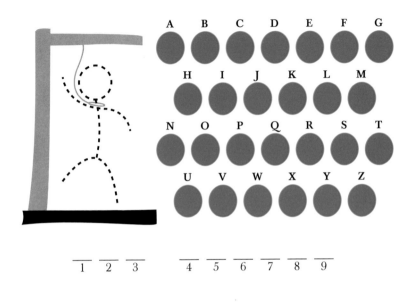

$$\overline{}_1 \quad \overline{}_2 \quad \overline{}_3 \qquad \overline{}_4 \quad \overline{}_5 \quad \overline{}_6 \quad \overline{}_7 \quad \overline{}_8 \quad \overline{}_9$$

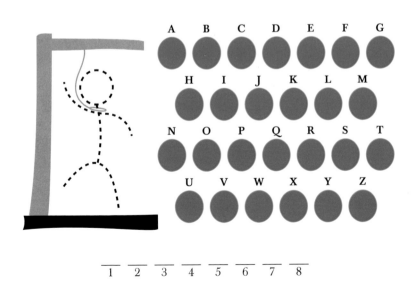

$$\overline{}_1 \quad \overline{}_2 \quad \overline{}_3 \quad \overline{}_4 \quad \overline{}_5 \quad \overline{}_6 \quad \overline{}_7 \quad \overline{}_8$$

79

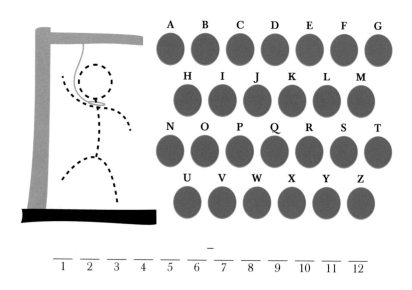

$$\overline{}_{1} \quad \overline{}_{2} \quad \overline{}_{3} \quad \overline{}_{4} \quad \overline{}_{5} \quad \overline{}_{6} \quad \overline{-}_{7} \quad \overline{}_{8} \quad \overline{}_{9} \quad \overline{}_{10} \quad \overline{}_{11} \quad \overline{}_{12}$$

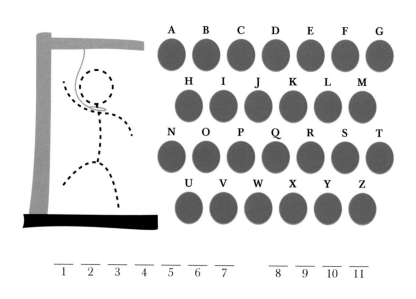

$$\overline{}_{1} \quad \overline{}_{2} \quad \overline{}_{3} \quad \overline{}_{4} \quad \overline{}_{5} \quad \overline{}_{6} \quad \overline{}_{7} \qquad \overline{}_{8} \quad \overline{}_{9} \quad \overline{}_{10} \quad \overline{}_{11}$$

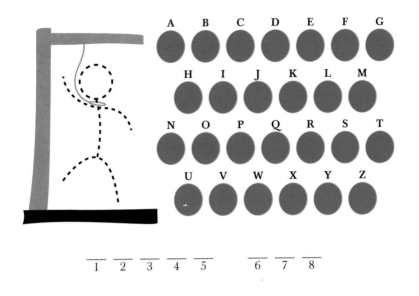

A B C D E F G
H I J K L M
N O P Q R S T
U V W X Y Z

$\overline{1}$ $\overline{2}$ $\overline{3}$ $\overline{4}$ $\overline{5}$ $\quad$ $\overline{6}$ $\overline{7}$ $\overline{8}$

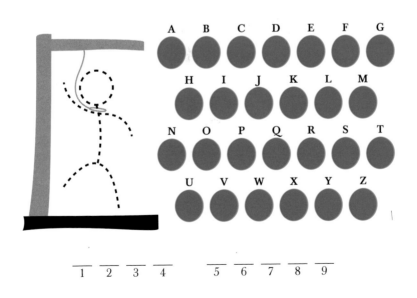

A B C D E F G
H I J K L M
N O P Q R S T
U V W X Y Z

$\overline{1}$ $\overline{2}$ $\overline{3}$ $\overline{4}$ $\quad$ $\overline{5}$ $\overline{6}$ $\overline{7}$ $\overline{8}$ $\overline{9}$

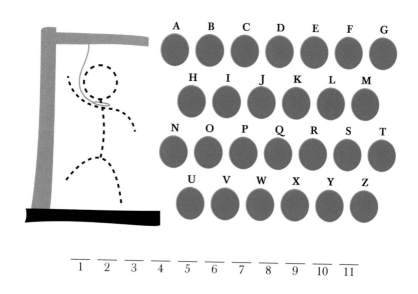

A B C D E F G
H I J K L M
N O P Q R S T
U V W X Y Z

$\overline{}$ $\overline{}$ $\overline{}$ $\overline{}$ $\overline{}$ $\overline{}$ $\overline{}$ $\overline{}$ $\overline{}$ $\overline{}$ $\overline{}$
1 2 3 4 5 6 7 8 9 10 11

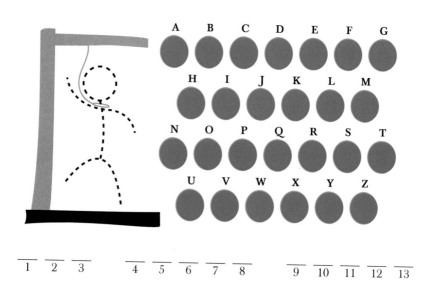

A B C D E F G
H I J K L M
N O P Q R S T
U V W X Y Z

$\overline{}$ $\overline{}$ $\overline{}$ $\quad$ $\overline{}$ $\overline{}$ $\overline{}$ $\overline{}$ $\overline{}$ $\quad$ $\overline{}$ $\overline{}$ $\overline{}$ $\overline{}$ $\overline{}$
1 2 3 4 5 6 7 8 9 10 11 12 13

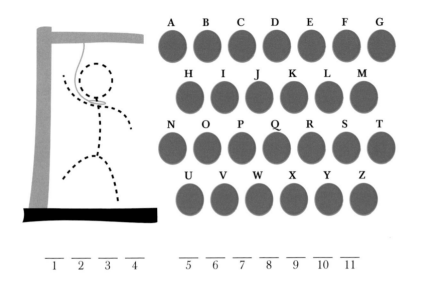

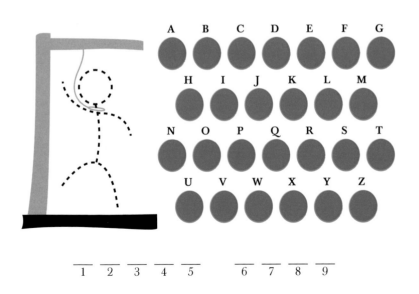

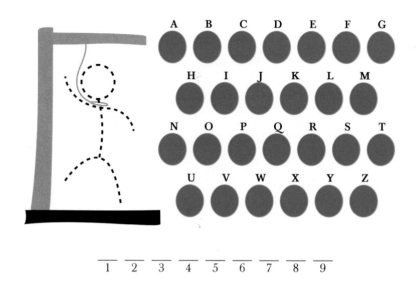

A B C D E F G
H I J K L M
N O P Q R S T
U V W X Y Z

$\overline{1}$ $\overline{2}$ $\overline{3}$ $\overline{4}$ $\overline{5}$ $\overline{6}$ $\overline{7}$ $\overline{8}$ $\overline{9}$

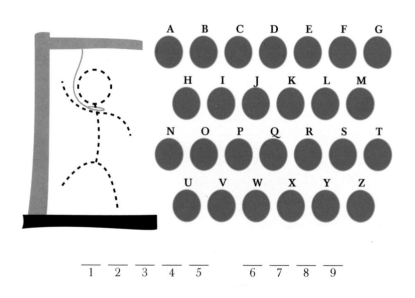

A B C D E F G
H I J K L M
N O P Q R S T
U V W X Y Z

$\overline{1}$ $\overline{2}$ $\overline{3}$ $\overline{4}$ $\overline{5}$ $\quad$ $\overline{6}$ $\overline{7}$ $\overline{8}$ $\overline{9}$

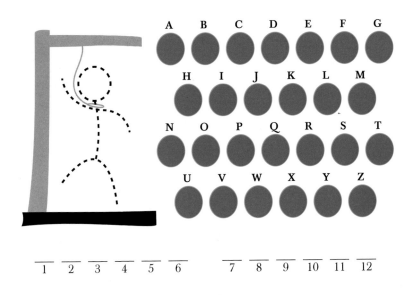

A B C D E F G
H I J K L M
N O P Q R S T
U V W X Y Z

$\overline{}_1 \overline{}_2 \overline{}_3 \overline{}_4 \overline{}_5 \overline{}_6 \qquad \overline{}_7 \overline{}_8 \overline{}_9 \overline{}_{10} \overline{}_{11} \overline{}_{12}$

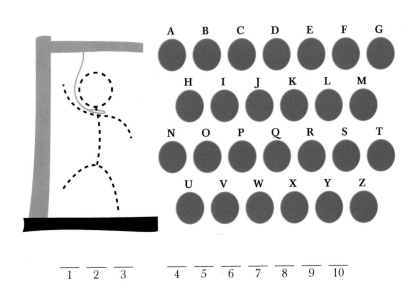

A B C D E F G
H I J K L M
N O P Q R S T
U V W X Y Z

$\overline{}_1 \overline{}_2 \overline{}_3 \qquad \overline{}_4 \overline{}_5 \overline{}_6 \overline{}_7 \overline{}_8 \overline{}_9 \overline{}_{10}$

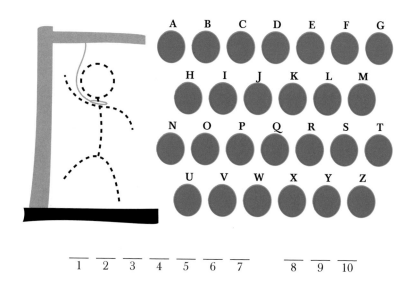

A B C D E F G
H I J K L M
N O P Q R S T
U V W X Y Z

$\overline{\quad}$ $\overline{\quad}$ $\overline{\quad}$ $\overline{\quad}$ $\overline{\quad}$ $\overline{\quad}$ $\overline{\quad}$ $\overline{\quad}$ $\overline{\quad}$ $\overline{\quad}$
1 2 3 4 5 6 7 8 9 10

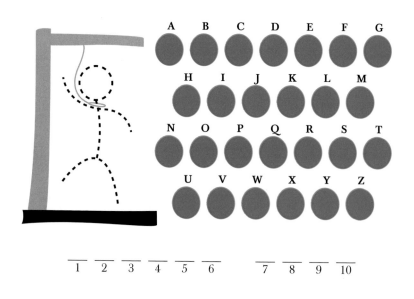

A B C D E F G
H I J K L M
N O P Q R S T
U V W X Y Z

$\overline{\quad}$ $\overline{\quad}$ $\overline{\quad}$ $\overline{\quad}$ $\overline{\quad}$ $\overline{\quad}$ $\overline{\quad}$ $\overline{\quad}$ $\overline{\quad}$ $\overline{\quad}$
1 2 3 4 5 6 7 8 9 10

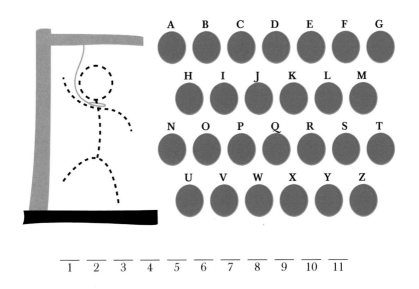

A B C D E F G
H I J K L M
N O P Q R S T
U V W X Y Z

$\overline{1}$ $\overline{2}$ $\overline{3}$ $\overline{4}$ $\overline{5}$ $\overline{6}$ $\overline{7}$ $\overline{8}$ $\overline{9}$ $\overline{10}$ $\overline{11}$

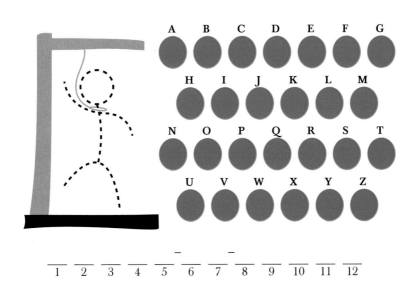

A B C D E F G
H I J K L M
N O P Q R S T
U V W X Y Z

$\overline{1}$ $\overline{2}$ $\overline{3}$ $\overline{4}$ $\overline{5}$ $\overline{6}$ $\overline{7}$ $\overline{8}$ $\overline{9}$ $\overline{10}$ $\overline{11}$ $\overline{12}$

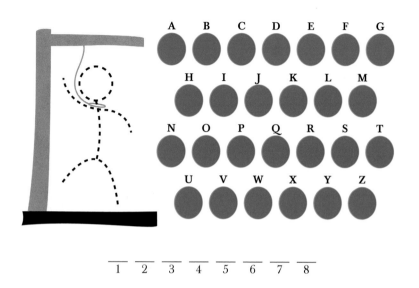

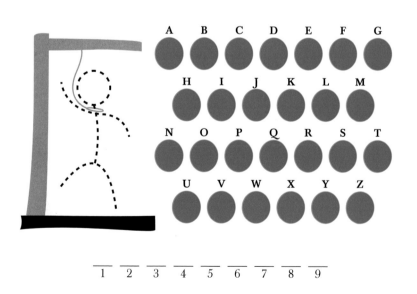

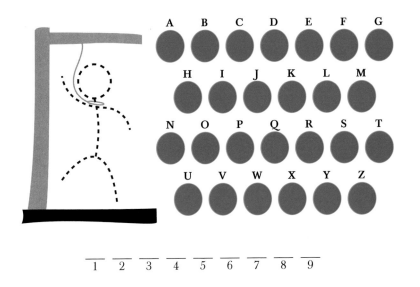

A	B	C	D	E	F	G

H	I	J	K	L	M

N	O	P	Q	R	S	T

U	V	W	X	Y	Z

$$\overline{1} \ \overline{2} \ \overline{3} \ \overline{4} \ \overline{5} \ \overline{6} \ \overline{7} \ \overline{8} \ \overline{9}$$

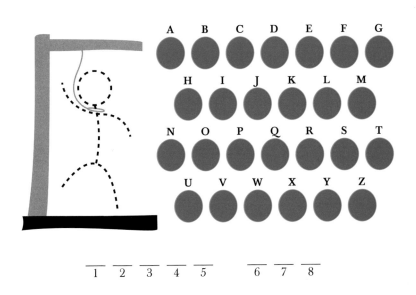

A	B	C	D	E	F	G

H	I	J	K	L	M

N	O	P	Q	R	S	T

U	V	W	X	Y	Z

$$\overline{1} \ \overline{2} \ \overline{3} \ \overline{4} \ \overline{5} \qquad \overline{6} \ \overline{7} \ \overline{8}$$

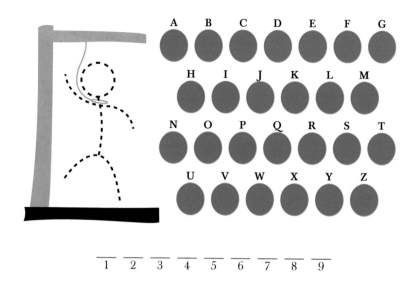

$\overline{1}$ $\overline{2}$ $\overline{3}$ $\overline{4}$ $\overline{5}$ $\overline{6}$ $\overline{7}$ $\overline{8}$ $\overline{9}$

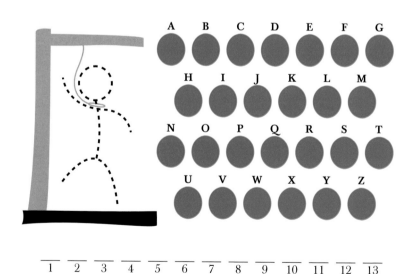

$\overline{1}$ $\overline{2}$ $\overline{3}$ $\overline{4}$ $\overline{5}$ $\overline{6}$ $\overline{7}$ $\overline{8}$ $\overline{9}$ $\overline{10}$ $\overline{11}$ $\overline{12}$ $\overline{13}$

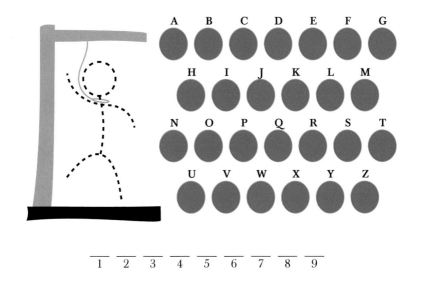

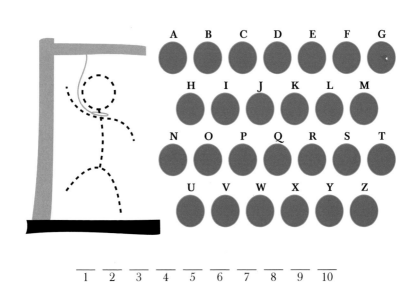

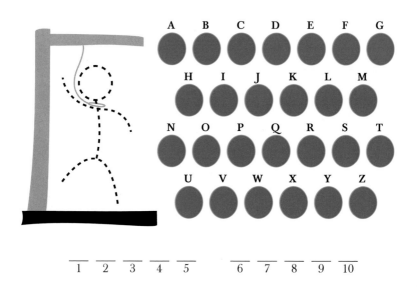

$$\overline{}_{1} \ \overline{}_{2} \ \overline{}_{3} \ \overline{}_{4} \ \overline{}_{5} \qquad \overline{}_{6} \ \overline{}_{7} \ \overline{}_{8} \ \overline{}_{9} \ \overline{}_{10}$$

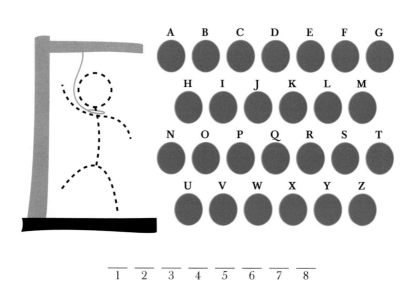

$$\overline{}_{1} \ \overline{}_{2} \ \overline{}_{3} \ \overline{}_{4} \ \overline{}_{5} \ \overline{}_{6} \ \overline{}_{7} \ \overline{}_{8}$$

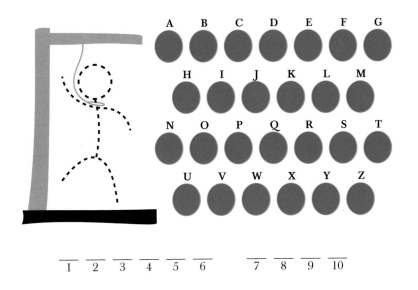

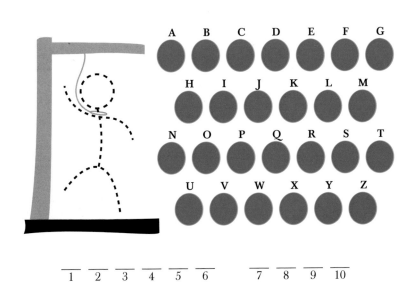

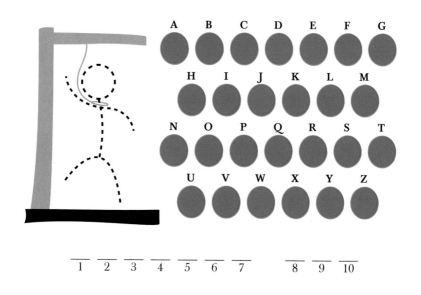

A B C D E F G

H I J K L M

N O P Q R S T

U V W X Y Z

$\overline{\ \ }$ $\overline{\ \ }$ $\overline{\ \ }$ $\overline{\ \ }$ $\overline{\ \ }$ $\overline{\ \ }$ $\overline{\ \ }$ $\overline{\ \ }$ $\overline{\ \ }$ $\overline{\ \ }$
1   2   3   4   5   6   7   8   9 10

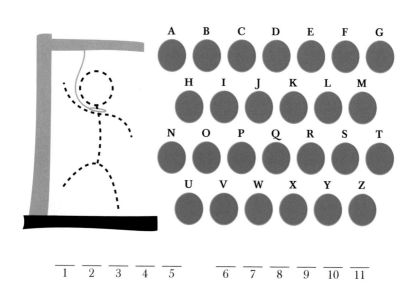

A B C D E F G

H I J K L M

N O P Q R S T

U V W X Y Z

1   2   3   4   5   6   7   8   9 10 11

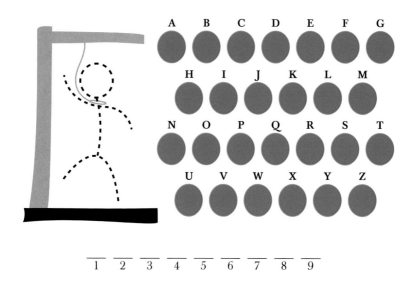

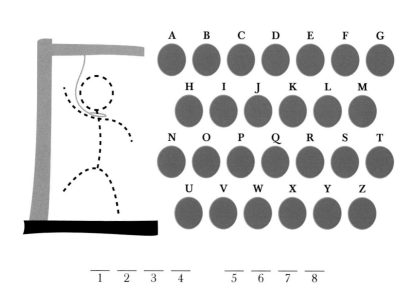

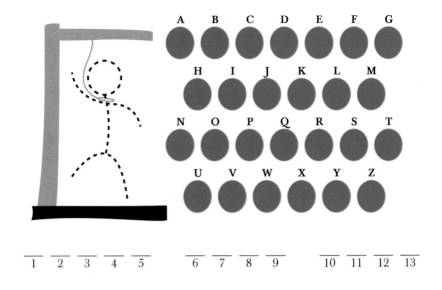

A B C D E F G
H I J K L M
N O P Q R S T
U V W X Y Z

$\overline{}_1 \overline{}_2 \overline{}_3 \overline{}_4 \overline{}_5 \quad \overline{}_6 \overline{}_7 \overline{}_8 \overline{}_9 \quad \overline{}_{10} \overline{}_{11} \overline{}_{12} \overline{}_{13}$

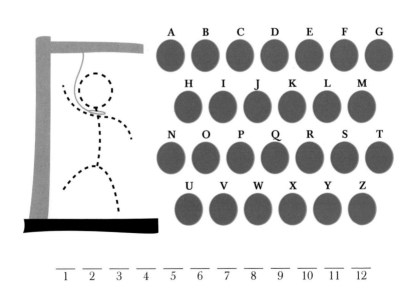

A B C D E F G
H I J K L M
N O P Q R S T
U V W X Y Z

$\overline{}_1 \overline{}_2 \overline{}_3 \overline{}_4 \overline{}_5 \overline{}_6 \overline{}_7 \overline{}_8 \overline{}_9 \overline{}_{10} \overline{}_{11} \overline{}_{12}$

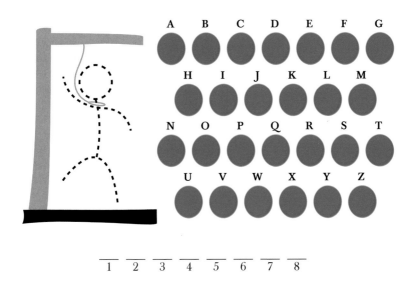

A B C D E F G

H I J K L M

N O P Q R S T

U V W X Y Z

__ __ __ __ __ __ __ __
1 2 3 4 5 6 7 8

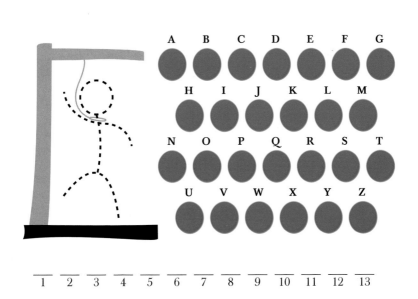

A B C D E F G

H I J K L M

N O P Q R S T

U V W X Y Z

__ __ __ __ __ __ __ __ __ __ __ __ __
1 2 3 4 5 6 7 8 9 10 11 12 13

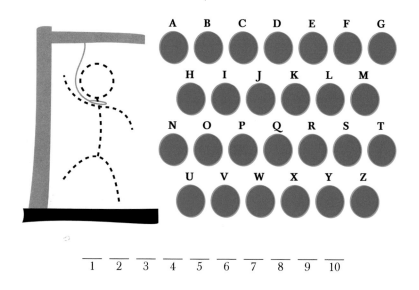

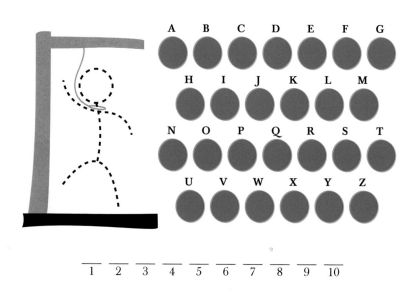

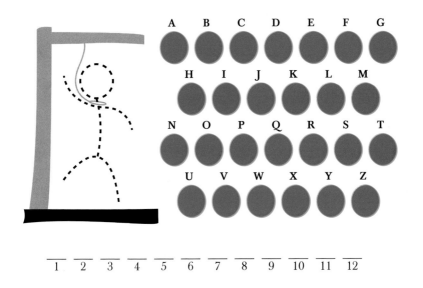

A B C D E F G
H I J K L M
N O P Q R S T
U V W X Y Z

‾1‾ ‾2‾ ‾3‾ ‾4‾ ‾5‾ ‾6‾ ‾7‾ ‾8‾ ‾9‾ ‾10‾ ‾11‾ ‾12‾

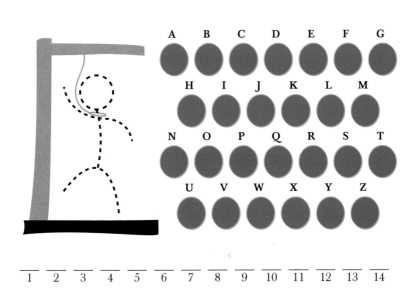

A B C D E F G
H I J K L M
N O P Q R S T
U V W X Y Z

‾1‾ ‾2‾ ‾3‾ ‾4‾ ‾5‾ ‾6‾ ‾7‾ ‾8‾ ‾9‾ ‾10‾ ‾11‾ ‾12‾ ‾13‾ ‾14‾

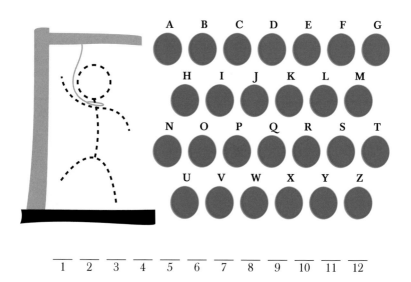

A B C D E F G
H I J K L M
N O P Q R S T
U V W X Y Z

$\overline{}$ $\overline{}$ $\overline{}$ $\overline{}$ $\overline{}$ $\overline{}$ $\overline{}$ $\overline{}$ $\overline{}$ $\overline{}$ $\overline{}$ $\overline{}$
1 2 3 4 5 6 7 8 9 10 11 12

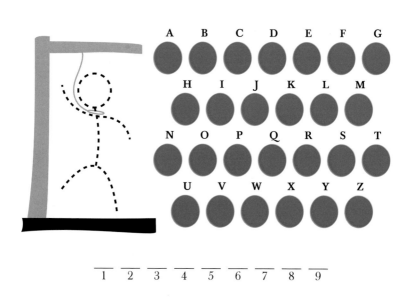

A B C D E F G
H I J K L M
N O P Q R S T
U V W X Y Z

$\overline{}$ $\overline{}$ $\overline{}$ $\overline{}$ $\overline{}$ $\overline{}$ $\overline{}$ $\overline{}$ $\overline{}$
1 2 3 4 5 6 7 8 9

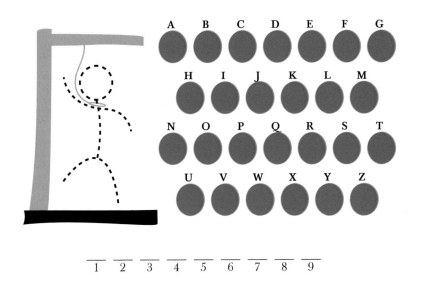

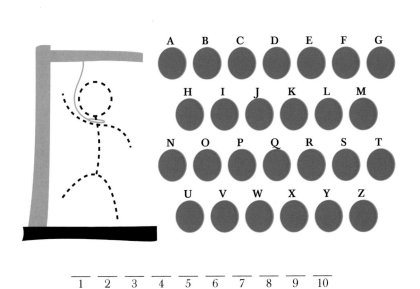

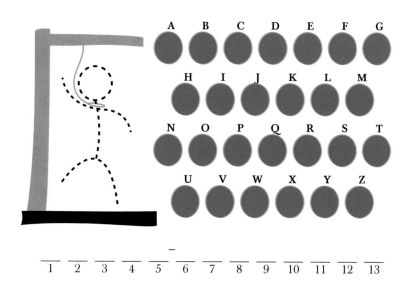

A B C D E F G
H I J K L M
N O P Q R S T
U V W X Y Z

$$\overline{}_{1} \ \overline{}_{2} \ \overline{}_{3} \ \overline{}_{4} \ \overline{-}_{5} \ \overline{}_{6} \ \overline{}_{7} \ \overline{}_{8} \ \overline{}_{9} \ \overline{}_{10} \ \overline{}_{11} \ \overline{}_{12} \ \overline{}_{13}$$

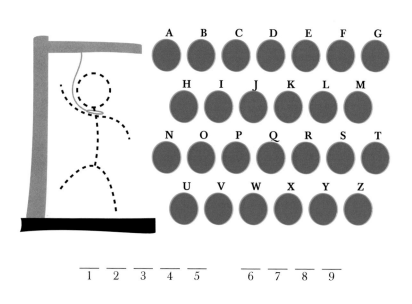

A B C D E F G
H I J K L M
N O P Q R S T
U V W X Y Z

$$\overline{}_{1} \ \overline{}_{2} \ \overline{}_{3} \ \overline{}_{4} \ \overline{}_{5} \qquad \overline{}_{6} \ \overline{}_{7} \ \overline{}_{8} \ \overline{}_{9}$$

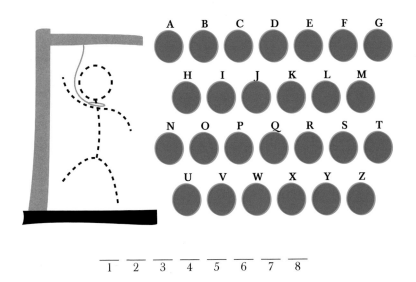

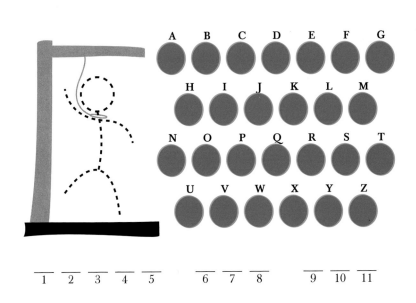

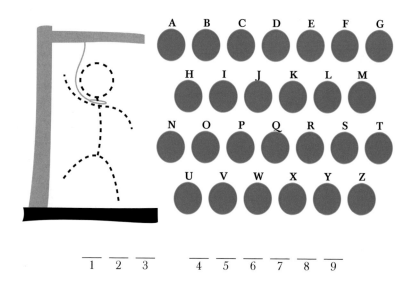

A B C D E F G
H I J K L M
N O P Q R S T
U V W X Y Z

$\overline{}_1$ $\overline{}_2$ $\overline{}_3$ $\overline{}_4$ $\overline{}_5$ $\overline{}_6$ $\overline{}_7$ $\overline{}_8$ $\overline{}_9$

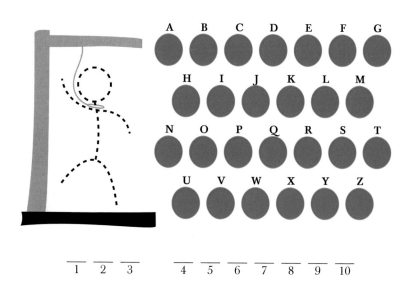

A B C D E F G
H I J K L M
N O P Q R S T
U V W X Y Z

$\overline{}_1$ $\overline{}_2$ $\overline{}_3$ $\overline{}_4$ $\overline{}_5$ $\overline{}_6$ $\overline{}_7$ $\overline{}_8$ $\overline{}_9$ $\overline{}_{10}$

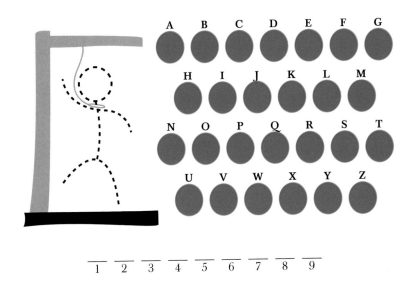

A B C D E F G
H I J K L M
N O P Q R S T
U V W X Y Z

$\overline{}_1 \ \overline{}_2 \ \overline{}_3 \ \overline{}_4 \ \overline{}_5 \ \overline{}_6 \ \overline{}_7 \ \overline{}_8 \ \overline{}_9$

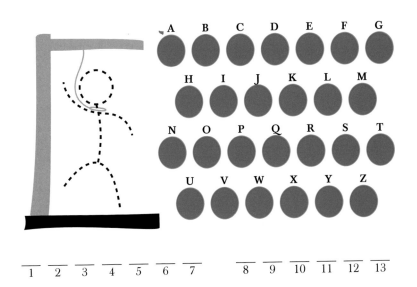

A B C D E F G
H I J K L M
N O P Q R S T
U V W X Y Z

$\overline{}_1 \ \overline{}_2 \ \overline{}_3 \ \overline{}_4 \ \overline{}_5 \ \overline{}_6 \ \overline{}_7 \qquad \overline{}_8 \ \overline{}_9 \ \overline{}_{10} \ \overline{}_{11} \ \overline{}_{12} \ \overline{}_{13}$

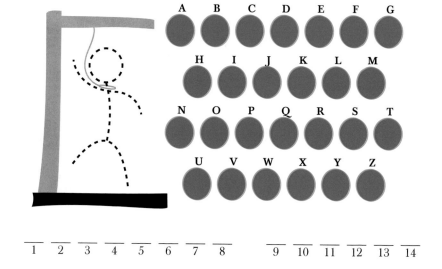

$\overline{}_{1}$ $\overline{}_{2}$ $\overline{}_{3}$ $\overline{}_{4}$ $\overline{}_{5}$ $\overline{}_{6}$ $\overline{}_{7}$ $\overline{}_{8}$ $\overline{}_{9}$ $\overline{}_{10}$ $\overline{}_{11}$ $\overline{}_{12}$ $\overline{}_{13}$ $\overline{}_{14}$

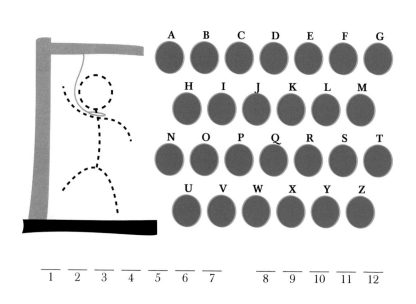

$\overline{}_{1}$ $\overline{}_{2}$ $\overline{}_{3}$ $\overline{}_{4}$ $\overline{}_{5}$ $\overline{}_{6}$ $\overline{}_{7}$ $\overline{}_{8}$ $\overline{}_{9}$ $\overline{}_{10}$ $\overline{}_{11}$ $\overline{}_{12}$

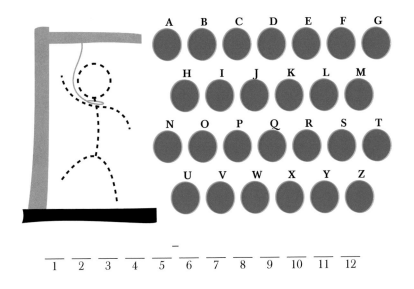

A	B	C	D	E	F	G
H	I	J	K	L	M
N	O	P	Q	R	S	T
U	V	W	X	Y	Z

$$\overline{}\ \overline{}\ \overline{}\ \overline{}\ \overline{}\ \overline{-}\ \overline{}\ \overline{}\ \overline{}\ \overline{}\ \overline{}\ \overline{}$$
1 2 3 4 5 6 7 8 9 10 11 12

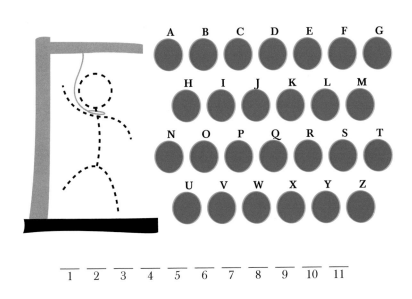

A	B	C	D	E	F	G
H	I	J	K	L	M
N	O	P	Q	R	S	T
U	V	W	X	Y	Z

1 2 3 4 5 6 7 8 9 10 11

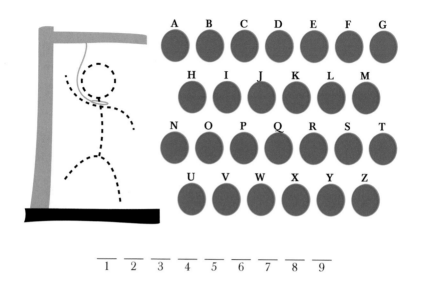

A B C D E F G
H I J K L M
N O P Q R S T
U V W X Y Z

— — — — — — — — —
1 2 3 4 5 6 7 8 9

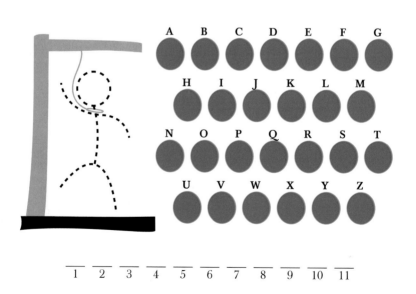

A B C D E F G
H I J K L M
N O P Q R S T
U V W X Y Z

— — — — — — — — — — —
1 2 3 4 5 6 7 8 9 10 11

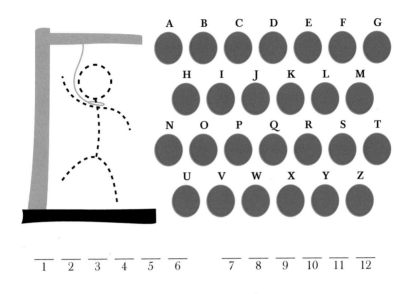

A B C D E F G
H I J K L M
N O P Q R S T
U V W X Y Z

$\overline{1}$ $\overline{2}$ $\overline{3}$ $\overline{4}$ $\overline{5}$ $\overline{6}$ $\qquad$ $\overline{7}$ $\overline{8}$ $\overline{9}$ $\overline{10}$ $\overline{11}$ $\overline{12}$

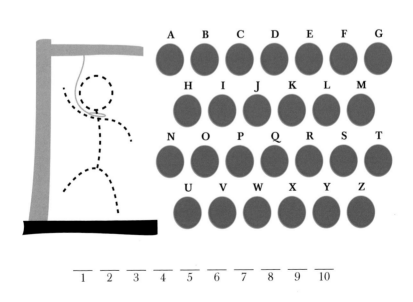

A B C D E F G
H I J K L M
N O P Q R S T
U V W X Y Z

$\overline{1}$ $\overline{2}$ $\overline{3}$ $\overline{4}$ $\overline{5}$ $\overline{6}$ $\overline{7}$ $\overline{8}$ $\overline{9}$ $\overline{10}$

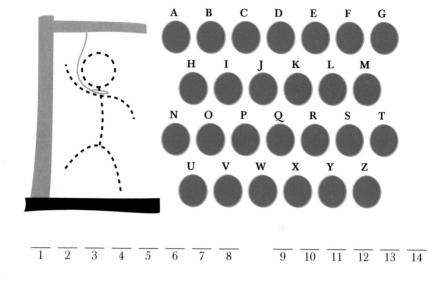

A	B	C	D	E	F	G
H	I	J	K	L	M	
N	O	P	Q	R	S	T
U	V	W	X	Y	Z	

$\overline{1}$ $\overline{2}$ $\overline{3}$ $\overline{4}$ $\overline{5}$ $\overline{6}$ $\overline{7}$ $\overline{8}$ $\overline{9}$ $\overline{10}$ $\overline{11}$ $\overline{12}$ $\overline{13}$ $\overline{14}$

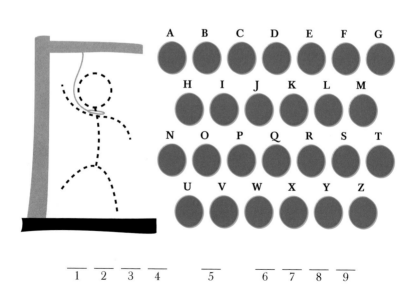

A	B	C	D	E	F	G
H	I	J	K	L	M	
N	O	P	Q	R	S	T
U	V	W	X	Y	Z	

$\overline{1}$ $\overline{2}$ $\overline{3}$ $\overline{4}$ $\overline{5}$ $\overline{6}$ $\overline{7}$ $\overline{8}$ $\overline{9}$

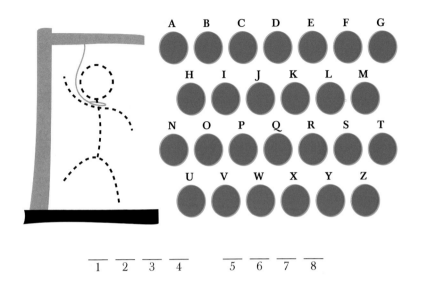

A B C D E F G
H I J K L M
N O P Q R S T
U V W X Y Z

$\overline{1}$ $\overline{2}$ $\overline{3}$ $\overline{4}$ $\overline{5}$ $\overline{6}$ $\overline{7}$ $\overline{8}$

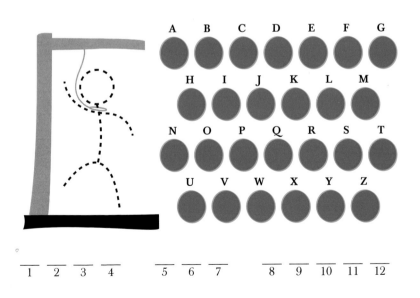

A B C D E F G
H I J K L M
N O P Q R S T
U V W X Y Z

$\overline{1}$ $\overline{2}$ $\overline{3}$ $\overline{4}$ $\overline{5}$ $\overline{6}$ $\overline{7}$ $\overline{8}$ $\overline{9}$ $\overline{10}$ $\overline{11}$ $\overline{12}$

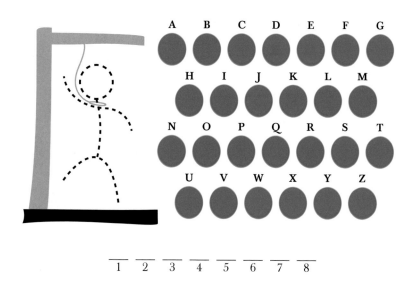

A B C D E F G
H I J K L M
N O P Q R S T
U V W X Y Z

$\overline{1}$ $\overline{2}$ $\overline{3}$ $\overline{4}$ $\overline{5}$ $\overline{6}$ $\overline{7}$ $\overline{8}$

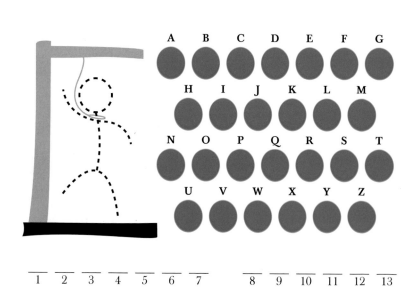

A B C D E F G
H I J K L M
N O P Q R S T
U V W X Y Z

$\overline{1}$ $\overline{2}$ $\overline{3}$ $\overline{4}$ $\overline{5}$ $\overline{6}$ $\overline{7}$ $\overline{8}$ $\overline{9}$ $\overline{10}$ $\overline{11}$ $\overline{12}$ $\overline{13}$

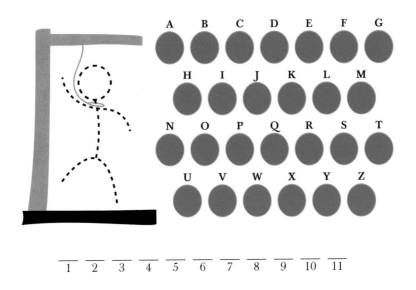

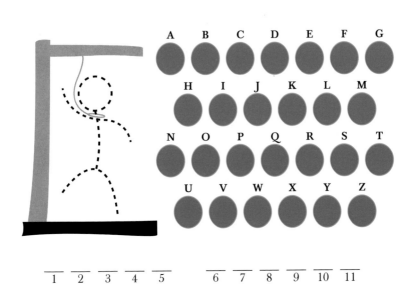

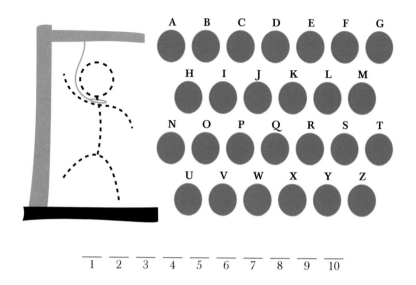

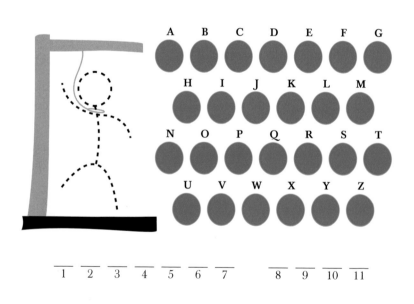

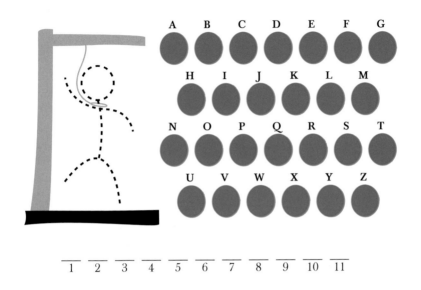

A B C D E F G
H I J K L M
N O P Q R S T
U V W X Y Z

$\overline{1}$ $\overline{2}$ $\overline{3}$ $\overline{4}$ $\overline{5}$ $\overline{6}$ $\overline{7}$ $\overline{8}$ $\overline{9}$ $\overline{10}$ $\overline{11}$

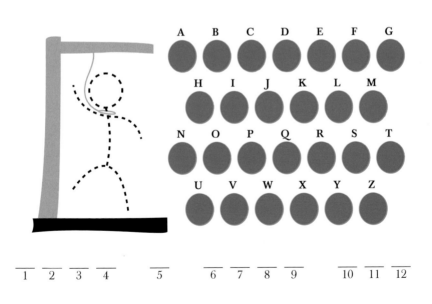

A B C D E F G
H I J K L M
N O P Q R S T
U V W X Y Z

$\overline{1}$ $\overline{2}$ $\overline{3}$ $\overline{4}$ $\overline{5}$ $\overline{6}$ $\overline{7}$ $\overline{8}$ $\overline{9}$ $\overline{10}$ $\overline{11}$ $\overline{12}$

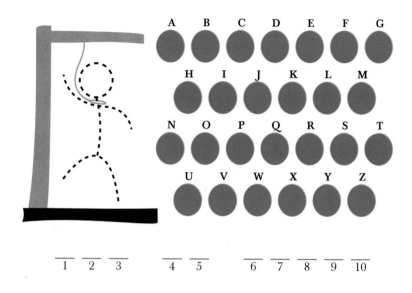

A B C D E F G
H I J K L M
N O P Q R S T
U V W X Y Z

$\overline{}_1$ $\overline{}_2$ $\overline{}_3$ $\overline{}_4$ $\overline{}_5$ $\overline{}_6$ $\overline{}_7$ $\overline{}_8$ $\overline{}_9$ $\overline{}_{10}$

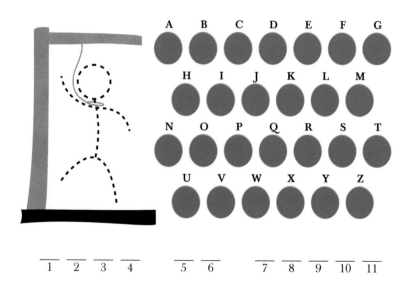

A B C D E F G
H I J K L M
N O P Q R S T
U V W X Y Z

$\overline{}_1$ $\overline{}_2$ $\overline{}_3$ $\overline{}_4$ $\overline{}_5$ $\overline{}_6$ $\overline{}_7$ $\overline{}_8$ $\overline{}_9$ $\overline{}_{10}$ $\overline{}_{11}$

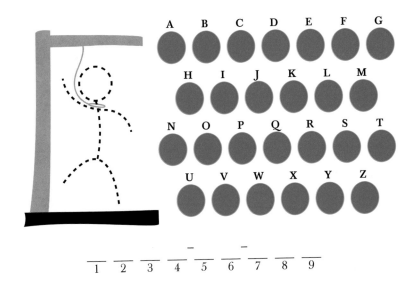

A B C D E F G
H I J K L M
N O P Q R S T
U V W X Y Z

$\overline{}_1$ $\overline{}_2$ $\overline{}_3$ $\overline{}_4$ $\overset{-}{\overline{}}_5$ $\overline{}_6$ $\overset{-}{\overline{}}_7$ $\overline{}_8$ $\overline{}_9$

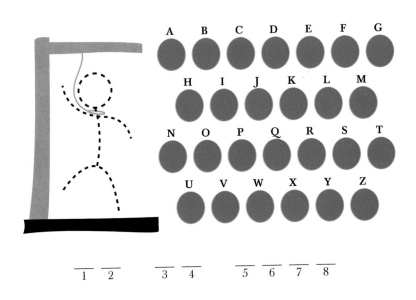

A B C D E F G
H I J K L M
N O P Q R S T
U V W X Y Z

$\overline{}_1$ $\overline{}_2$ $\overline{}_3$ $\overline{}_4$ $\overline{}_5$ $\overline{}_6$ $\overline{}_7$ $\overline{}_8$

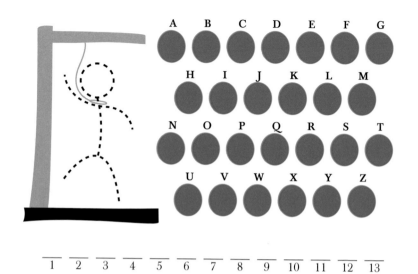

A B C D E F G
H I J K L M
N O P Q R S T
U V W X Y Z

$\overline{1}$ $\overline{2}$ $\overline{3}$ $\overline{4}$ $\overline{5}$ $\overline{6}$ $\overline{7}$ $\overline{8}$ $\overline{9}$ $\overline{10}$ $\overline{11}$ $\overline{12}$ $\overline{13}$

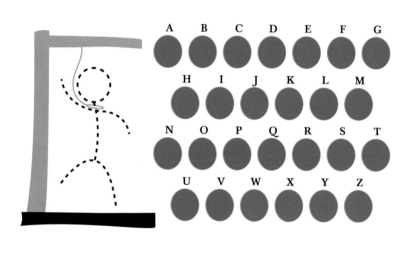

A B C D E F G
H I J K L M
N O P Q R S T
U V W X Y Z

$\overline{1}$ $\overline{2}$ $\overline{3}$ $\overline{4}$ $\overline{5}$ $\overline{6}$ $\overline{7}$ $\overline{8}$ $\overline{9}$ $\overline{10}$ $\overline{11}$ $\overline{12}$ $\overline{13}$ $\overline{14}$

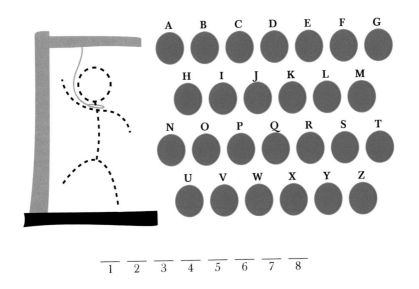

$$\overline{}_1 \quad \overline{}_2 \quad \overline{}_3 \quad \overline{}_4 \quad \overline{}_5 \quad \overline{}_6 \quad \overline{}_7 \quad \overline{}_8$$

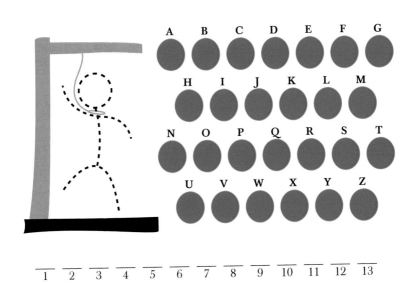

$$\overline{}_1 \quad \overline{}_2 \quad \overline{}_3 \quad \overline{}_4 \quad \overline{}_5 \quad \overline{}_6 \quad \overline{}_7 \quad \overline{}_8 \quad \overline{}_9 \quad \overline{}_{10} \quad \overline{}_{11} \quad \overline{}_{12} \quad \overline{}_{13}$$

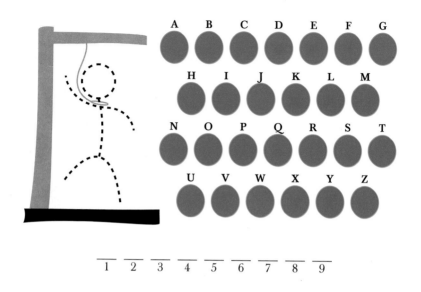

$$\overline{}_{1} \ \overline{}_{2} \ \overline{}_{3} \ \overline{}_{4} \ \overline{}_{5} \ \overline{}_{6} \ \overline{}_{7} \ \overline{}_{8} \ \overline{}_{9}$$

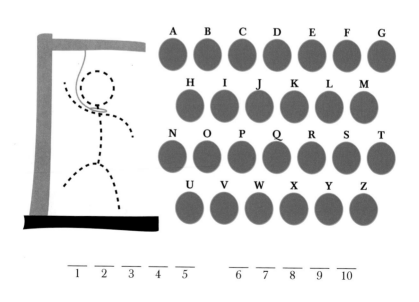

$$\overline{}_{1} \ \overline{}_{2} \ \overline{}_{3} \ \overline{}_{4} \ \overline{}_{5} \qquad \overline{}_{6} \ \overline{}_{7} \ \overline{}_{8} \ \overline{}_{9} \ \overline{}_{10}$$

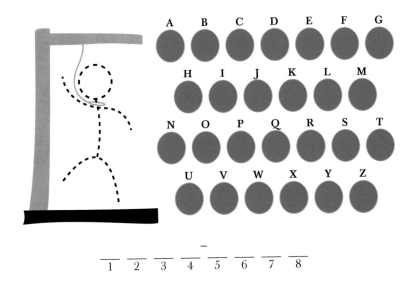

$$\overline{1} \ \overline{2} \ \overline{3} \ \overline{4} \ \overset{-}{\overline{5}} \ \overline{6} \ \overline{7} \ \overline{8}$$

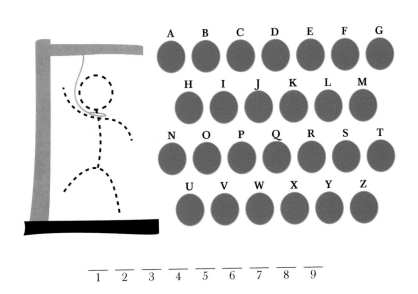

$$\overline{1} \ \overline{2} \ \overline{3} \ \overline{4} \ \overline{5} \ \overline{6} \ \overline{7} \ \overline{8} \ \overline{9}$$

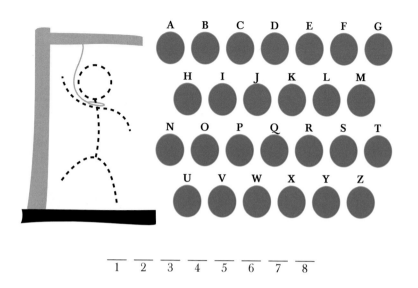

$$\overline{}_{1} \quad \overline{}_{2} \quad \overline{}_{3} \quad \overline{}_{4} \quad \overline{}_{5} \quad \overline{}_{6} \quad \overline{}_{7} \quad \overline{}_{8}$$

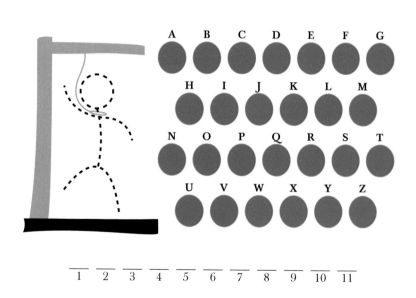

$$\overline{}_{1} \quad \overline{}_{2} \quad \overline{}_{3} \quad \overline{}_{4} \quad \overline{}_{5} \quad \overline{}_{6} \quad \overline{}_{7} \quad \overline{}_{8} \quad \overline{}_{9} \quad \overline{}_{10} \quad \overline{}_{11}$$

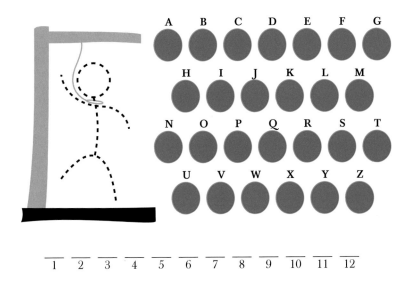

$$\overline{}_{1} \ \overline{}_{2} \ \overline{}_{3} \ \overline{}_{4} \ \overline{}_{5} \ \overline{}_{6} \ \overline{}_{7} \ \overline{}_{8} \ \overline{}_{9} \ \overline{}_{10} \ \overline{}_{11} \ \overline{}_{12}$$

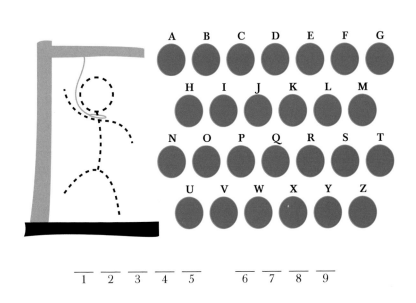

$$\overline{}_{1} \ \overline{}_{2} \ \overline{}_{3} \ \overline{}_{4} \ \overline{}_{5} \qquad \overline{}_{6} \ \overline{}_{7} \ \overline{}_{8} \ \overline{}_{9}$$

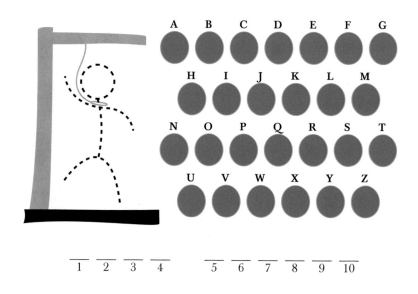

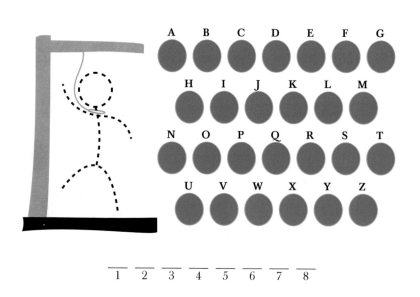

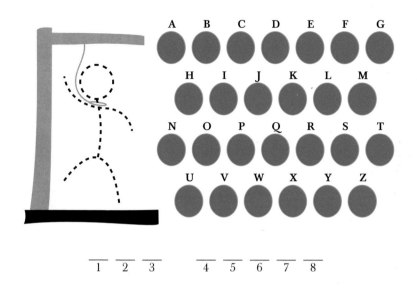

A B C D E F G
H I J K L M
N O P Q R S T
U V W X Y Z

$\overline{}$ 1 $\overline{}$ 2 $\overline{}$ 3　　$\overline{}$ 4 $\overline{}$ 5 $\overline{}$ 6 $\overline{}$ 7 $\overline{}$ 8

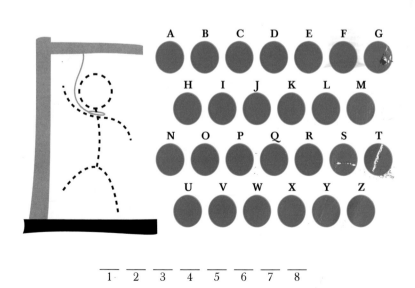

A B C D E F G
H I J K L M
N O P Q R S T
U V W X Y Z

$\overline{}$ 1 $\overline{}$ 2 $\overline{}$ 3 $\overline{}$ 4 $\overline{}$ 5 $\overline{}$ 6 $\overline{}$ 7 $\overline{}$ 8

125

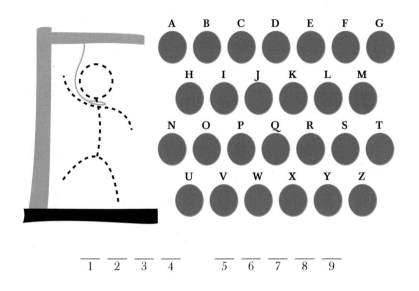

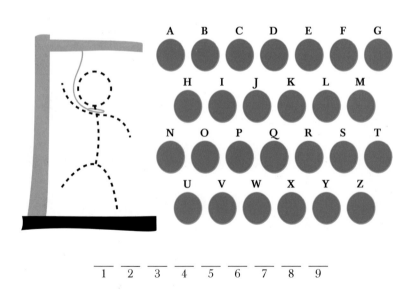

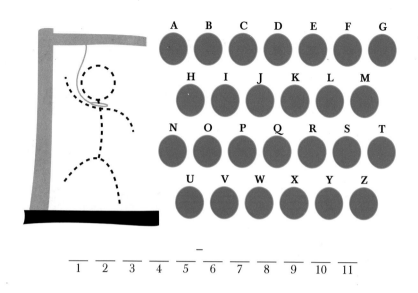

A B C D E F G
H I J K L M
N O P Q R S T
U V W X Y Z

$\overline{}$
$\overline{1}$ $\overline{2}$ $\overline{3}$ $\overline{4}$ $\overline{5}$ $\overline{6}$ $\overline{7}$ $\overline{8}$ $\overline{9}$ $\overline{10}$ $\overline{11}$

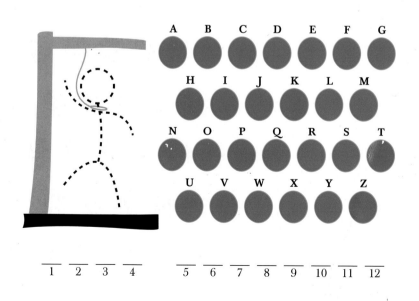

A B C D E F G
H I J K L M
N O P Q R S T
U V W X Y Z

$\overline{1}$ $\overline{2}$ $\overline{3}$ $\overline{4}$ $\overline{5}$ $\overline{6}$ $\overline{7}$ $\overline{8}$ $\overline{9}$ $\overline{10}$ $\overline{11}$ $\overline{12}$

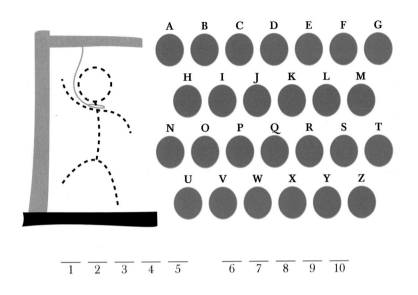

A B C D E F G
H I J K L M
N O P Q R S T
U V W X Y Z

$\overline{}_1\ \overline{}_2\ \overline{}_3\ \overline{}_4\ \overline{}_5\qquad \overline{}_6\ \overline{}_7\ \overline{}_8\ \overline{}_9\ \overline{}_{10}$

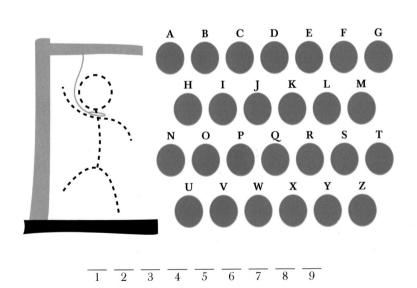

A B C D E F G
H I J K L M
N O P Q R S T
U V W X Y Z

$\overline{}_1\ \overline{}_2\ \overline{}_3\ \overline{}_4\ \overline{}_5\ \overline{}_6\ \overline{}_7\ \overline{}_8\ \overline{}_9$

127